AS **PE** for AQA

WORKBOOK

Nesta Wiggins-James • Rob James • Graham Thompson

Inspiring generations

Heinemann Educational Publishers
Halley Court, Jordan Hill, Oxford OX2 8EJ
Part of Harcourt Education

Heinemann is the registered trademark of
Harcourt Education Limited

© Harcourt Education 2005

First published 2005

10 09 08 07 06
10 9 8 7 6 5 4 3 2

British Library Cataloguing in Publication Data is available
from the British Library on request.

10-digit ISBN 0 435499 34 3
13-digit ISBN 978 0 435499 34 1

Typeset by 𝟋 Tek-Art, Croydon, Surrey
Original illustrations © Harcourt Education Limited, 2005
Printed by Scotprint
Cover photo: © Corbis

Acknowledgements
Every effort has been made to contact copyright holders of material
reproduced in this book. Any omissions will be rectified in subsequent
printings if notice is given to the publishers.

The photo on page 57 occurs courtesy of Topham Picture Point

AQA examination questions are reproduced by permission of the Assessment
and Qualifications Alliance.

Where sample answers and examiner's comments have been provided, these
are the responsibility of the author and have not been provided or approved
by AQA.

Contents

Unit 1: Physiological and psychological factors which improve performance

Chapter 1: Joints, muscles and mechanics – a study of human movement

1. Below is a diagram of the human skeleton. Complete by filling in the missing labels.

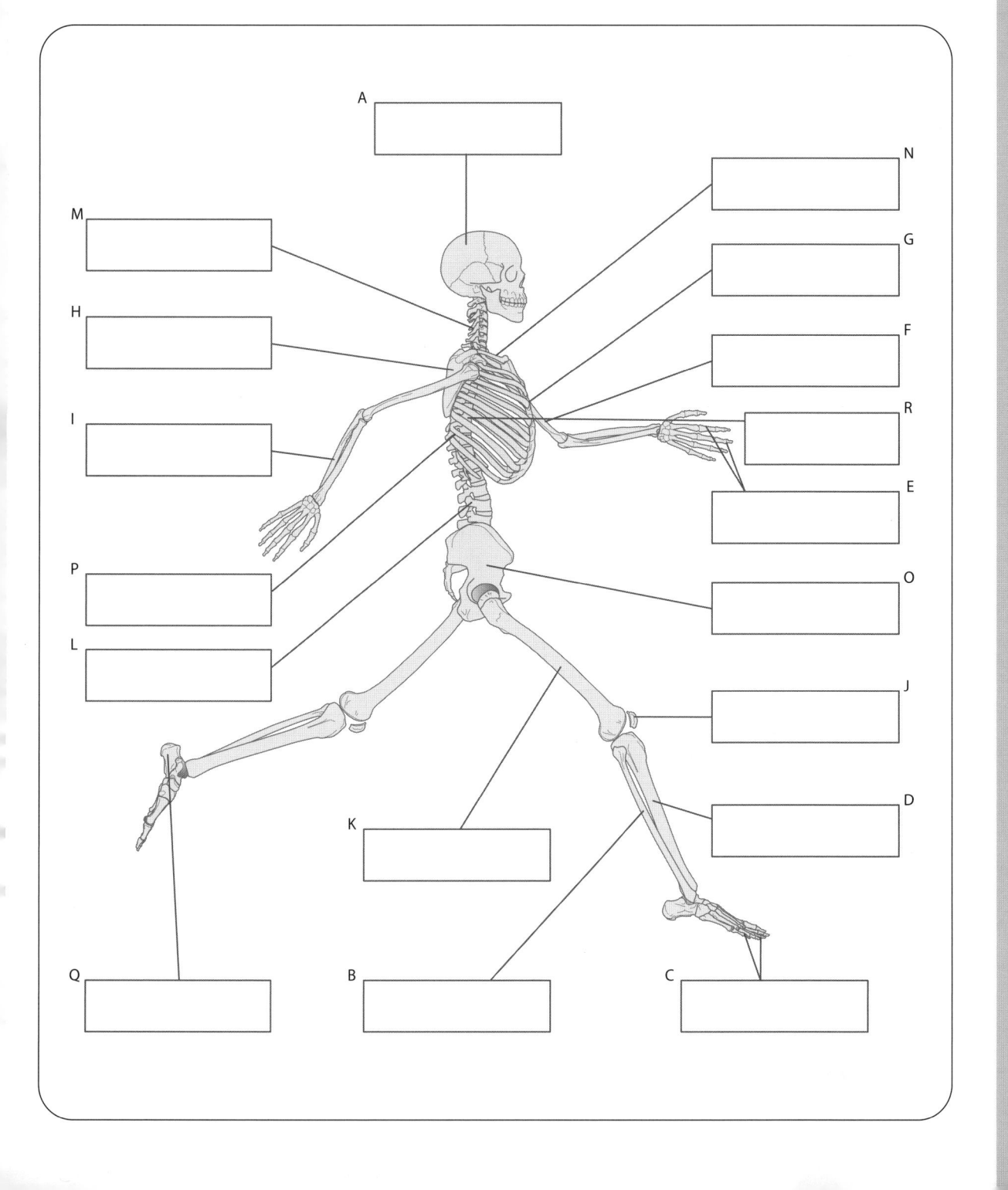

2. The table below identifies several features common to all synovial joints. Complete the table with the relevant definition and function of each structure.

Feature	Definition	Function
Joint capsule		
Articular cartilage		
Synovial fluid		
Synovial membrane		
Ligament		
Bursae		

3. Match the following terms with the correct definitions.

- *Appendicular skeleton*
- *Axial skeleton*
- *Fibrous joint*
- *Cartilaginous joint*
- *Synovial joint*

_____ A. The main axis of the body, which includes the bones of the skull, spine and rib cage.

_____ B. Joints which do not allow any movement, such as those between the plates of the skull.

_____ C. Joints which only allow a small degree of movement, such as those found between the vertebrae.

_____ D. The bones of the limbs together with the bones of the shoulder and hip girdles.

4. Complete the table below.

Joint	Type of joint	Articulating bones	Movements possible
Atlanto-axis			
Shoulder			
Elbow			
Radio-ulnar			
Wrist			

Joint	Type of joint	Articulating bones	Movements possible
Hip			
Knee			
Ankle			

5. Below is a diagram of the hip joint. Fill in the missing labels.

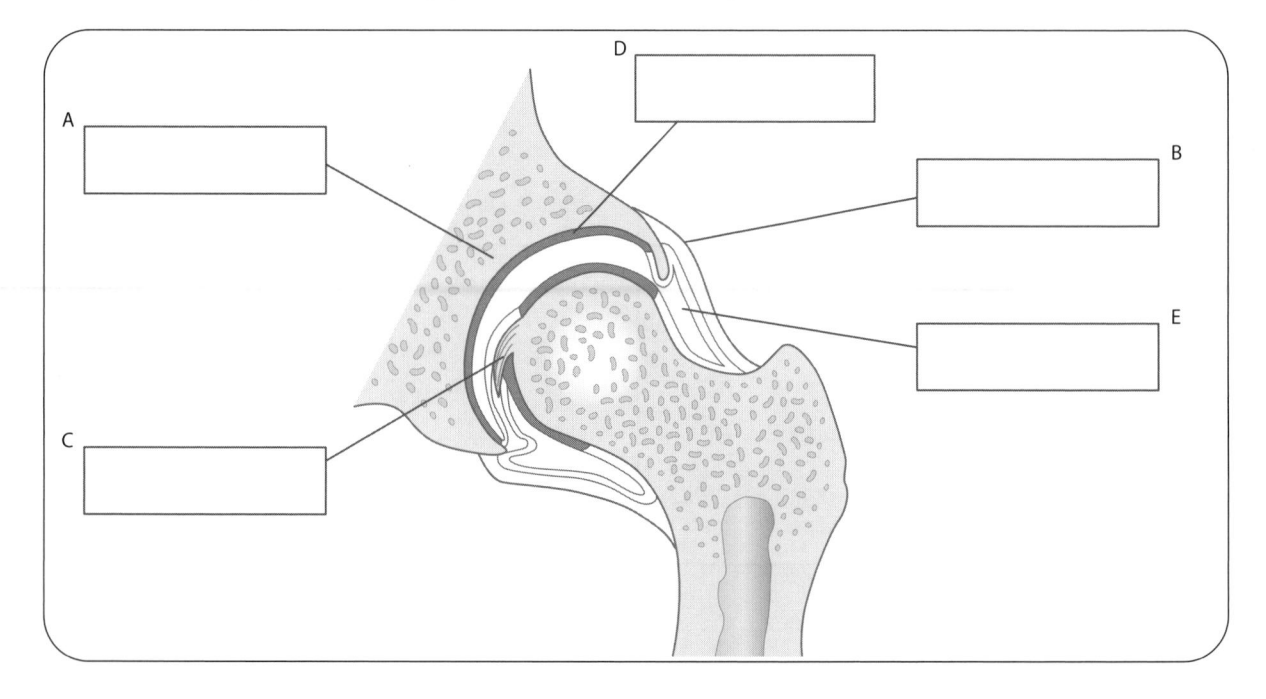

6. Below is a diagram featuring the muscles of the human body. Label the muscles indicated.

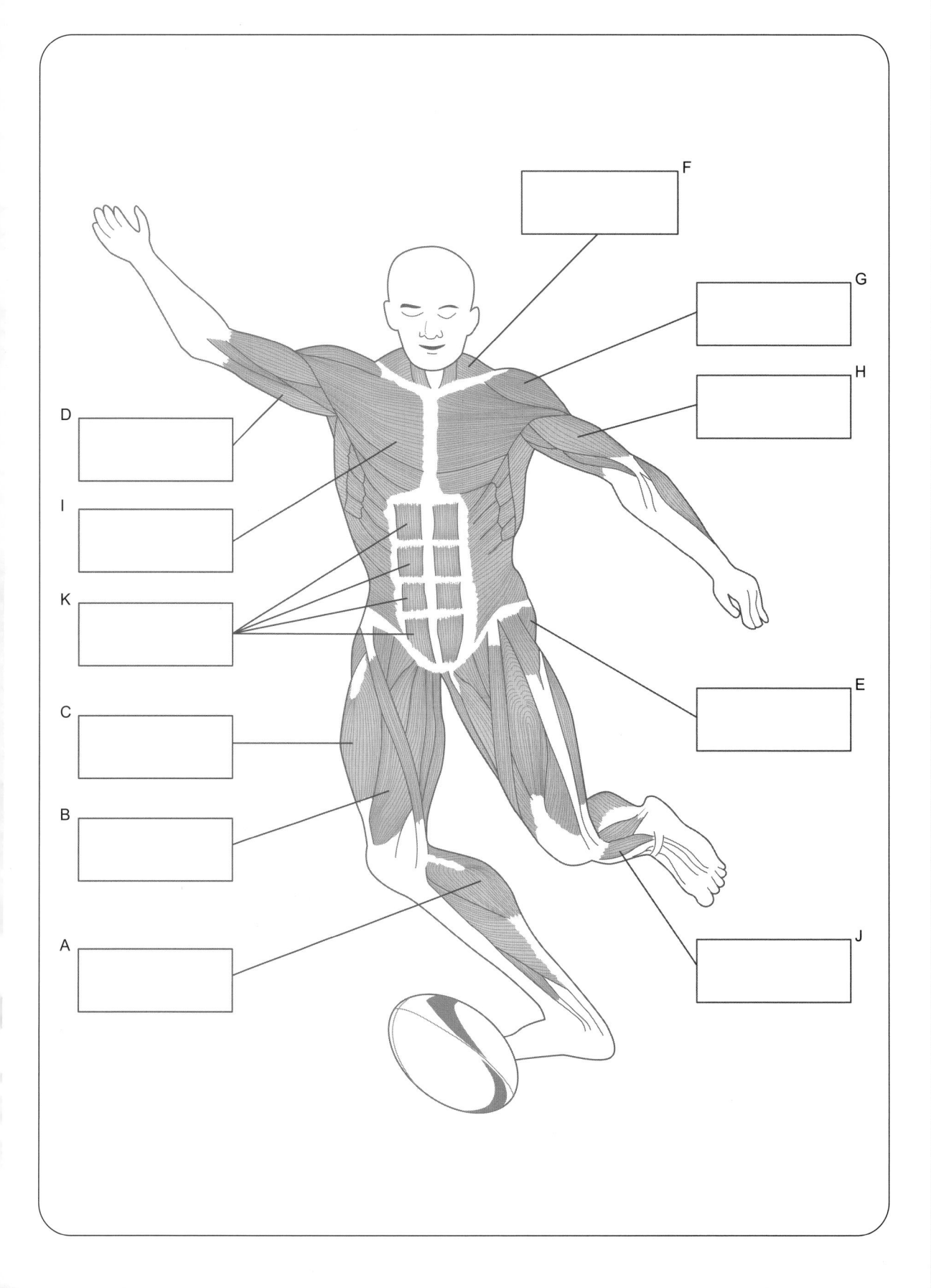

7. Complete the table below identifying the antagonistic action of the muscles at the hip joint.

Movement	Agonist	Antagonist	Fixator
Flexion			
Extension			
Abduction			
Adduction			
Medial rotation			
Lateral rotation			

8. Below is a diagram of the shoulder joint. Fill in the missing labels.

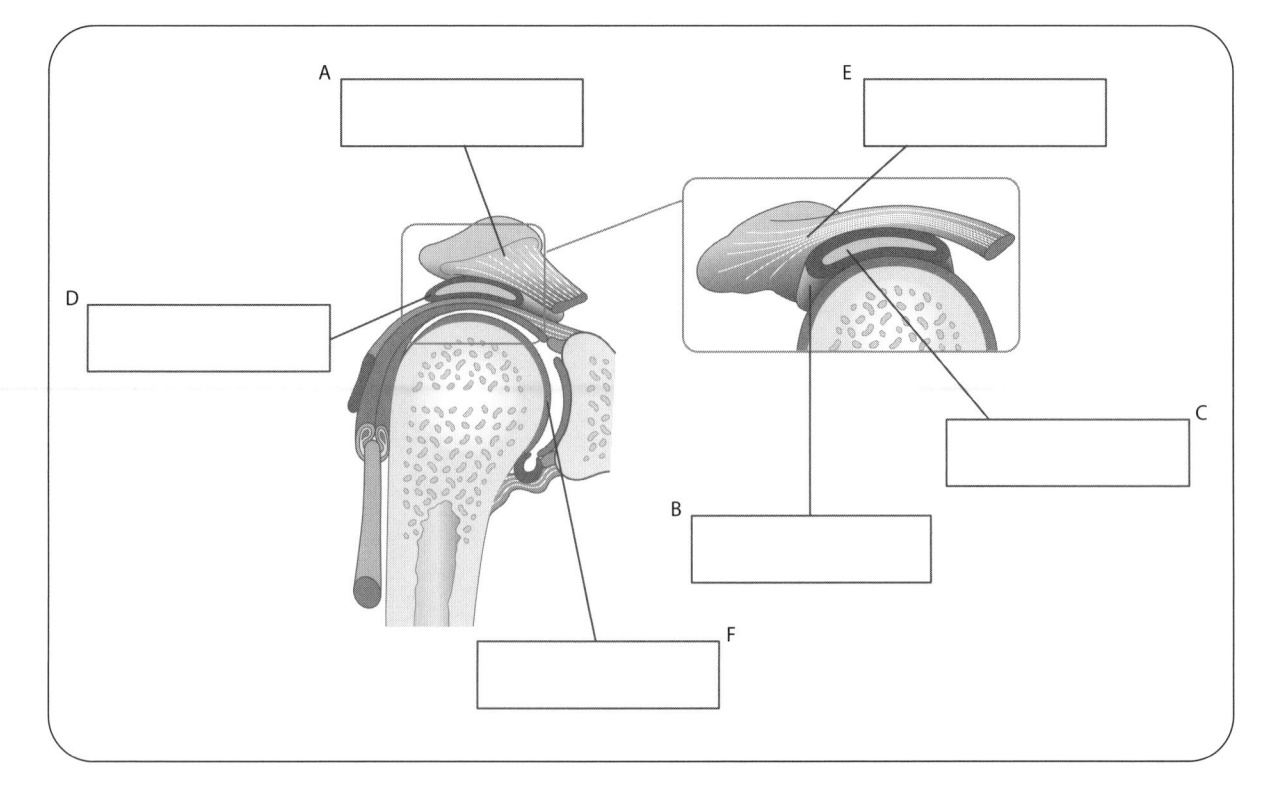

9. Complete the table below identifying the antagonistic action of the muscles at the shoulder joint.

Movement	Agonist	Antagonist	Fixator
Flexion			
Extension			
Horizontal flexion			
Horizontal extension			
Abduction			
Adduction			
Medial rotation			
Lateral rotation			

10. Explain what is meant by the origin and insertion of a muscle.

Origin: _____

_____

_____

Insertion: _____

_____

_____

11. Complete the table below giving the origin and insertion for each of the muscles stated.

Muscle	Origin	Insertion
Rectus femoris		
Biceps brachii		
Pectoralis major		
Gastrocnemius		
Triceps brachii		

12. Complete the passage by filling in the blanks using the words listed in the box. You may use some of the words more than once.

antagonistically   isometrically   agonists   eccentrically shortens   lengthening   concentric

Eccentric contraction occurs when a muscle contracts whilst _____. Concentric contraction occurs when a muscle _____ whilst contracting. During the upward phase of a press up, the triceps brachii are the main _____ at the elbow and the biceps brachii are working _____. The type of contraction taking place in the triceps brachii is _____ contraction.

During the downward phase of the press up, the triceps remain as the main _____ but this time contract _____. This controls the movement during the downward phase. When holding the press up in the down position, muscles acting on the elbows are working _____.

13. Complete the table below.

Movement pattern	Plane	Axis
Flexion/Extension		
Abduction/Adduction		
Medial/Lateral rotation		
Circumduction		
Plantarflexion/Dorsiflexion		
Pronation/Supination		

14. Fill in the missing gaps on lever systems.

In the human body the _____ act as levers and the _____ act as fulcra in order to enhance movement. There are three components to every lever system: an _____ force, a _____ force and a pivot or _____. There are three types or classes of lever: first, second and third class. In a first class lever the _____ lies between the _____ and the _____. An example of this in the human body is the _____. In a second class lever the _____ lies between the _____ and the _____. An example from sport when this lever system operates is _____

_____.

In a third class lever system the _____ lies between the _____ and the _____. This is the most popular class of lever system in the human body. An example from the sporting arena when a third class lever operates is _____ _____. The term mechanical disadvantage when applied to a lever system refers to _____

_____
_____.

Chapter 2: The cardiovascular system – the maintenance and control of blood supply

1. Using the diagram of the heart below, label the structures A–N.

- *Aorta*
- *Right atrium*
- *Left atrium*
- *Right ventricle*
- *Left ventricle*
- *Superior vena cava*
- *Pulmonary vein*
- *Pulmonary valve*
- *Aortic valve*
- *Tricuspid valve*
- *Bicuspid valve*
- *Inferior vena cava*
- *Pulmonary artery*
- *Septum*

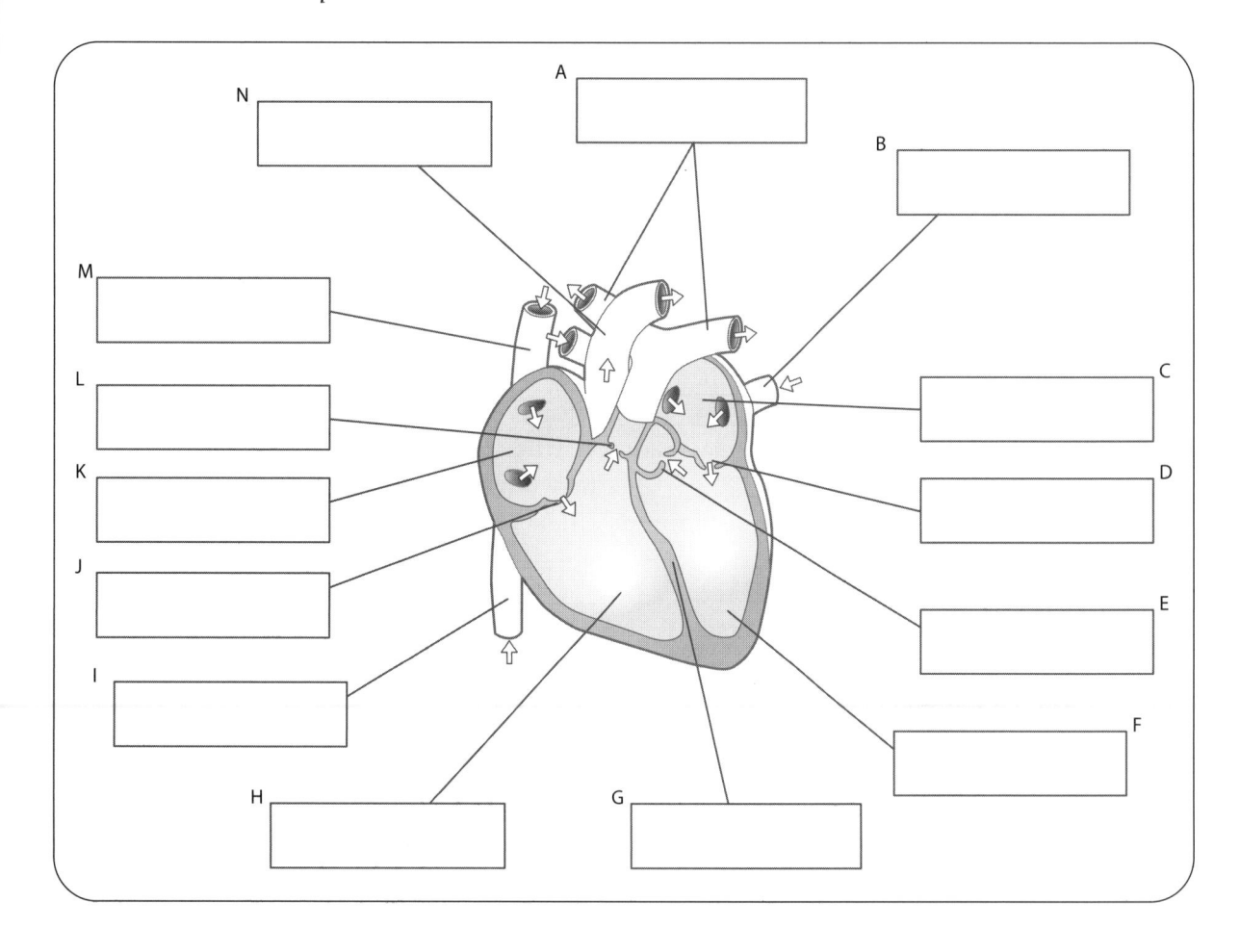

2. On the above diagram, colour the arrows blue that represent blood low in oxygen content; colour red those that represent oxygen-rich blood.

3. Starting at the venae cavae, place the following structures in the correct order that a red blood cell would pass on its journey through the heart.

- *Aorta*
- *Bicuspid valve*
- *Left atrium*
- *Left ventricle*
- *Lungs*
- *Pulmonary artery*
- *Pulmonary vein*
- *Right atrium*
- *Right ventricle*
- *Tricuspid valve*

a. *Venae cavae*

b. _____

c. _____

d. _____

e. _____

f. _____

g. _____

h. _____

i. _____

j. _____

k. _____

4. Match the following terms with the correct definition:

- *Atrioventricular Node (AVN)*
- *Bundle of His*
- *Pukinje (Purkyne) fibres*
- *Sinoatrial Node (SAN)*

_____ A. Specialized cardiac tissue that spreads a cardiac impulse throughout the myocardium, causing the ventricles to contract.

_____ B. A mass of specialized cardiac muscle fibres located in the right atrium and responsible for emitting the cardiac impulse. Also known as the pacemaker of the heart.

_____ C. A mass of conducting cells located in the right atrial wall, which acts as a distributor passing the cardiac impulse down through the septum.

_____ D. Two branches of the conduction system of the heart that run down the entire length of the septum.

5. Label the diagram of the conduction system of the heart with the appropriate terms from the following:

- *Atrioventricular Node (AVN)*
- *Bundle of His*
- *Pukinje (Purkyne) fibres*
- *Sinoatrial Node (SAN)*

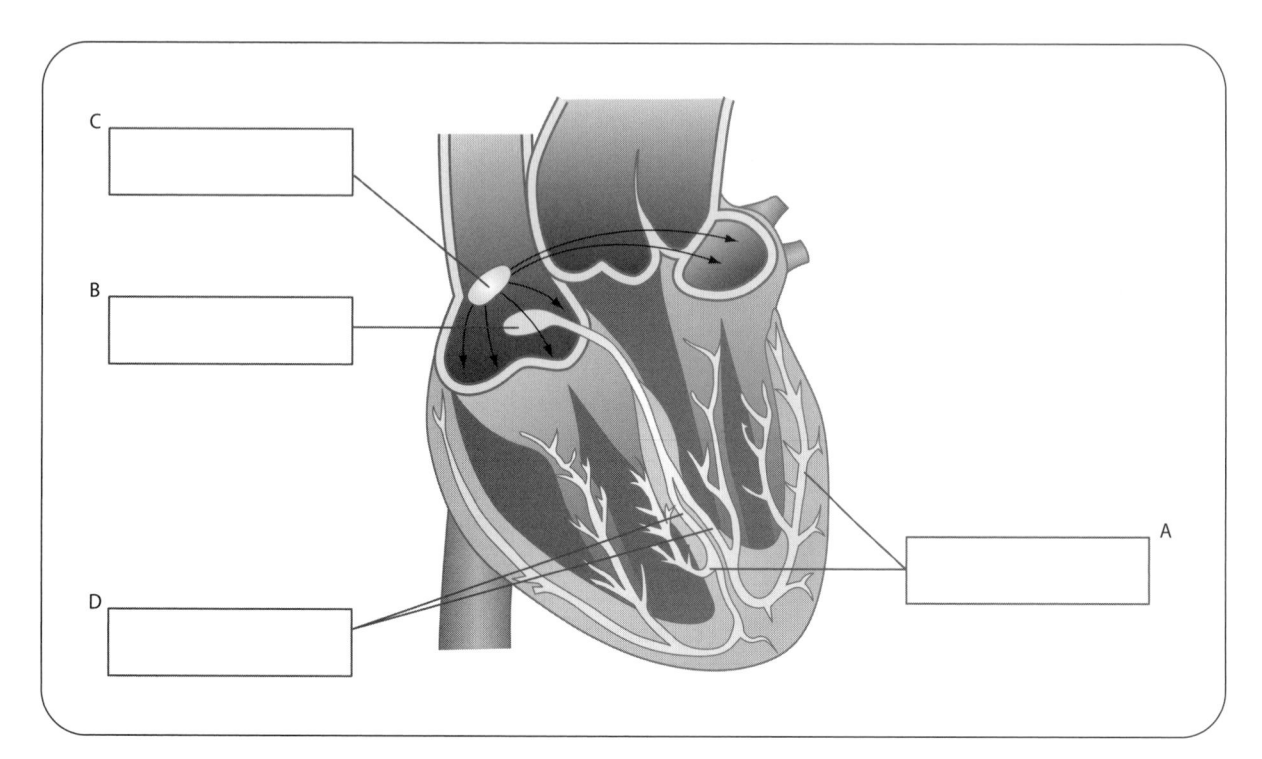

C

B

D

A

6. Fill in the missing gaps in the passage below with the appropriate words from the box.

atrial systole	ventricular systole	impulse	semi-lunar
atrial diastole	ventricular diastole	atrio-ventricular	SA

Each cardiac cycle begins with the generation of a cardiac _____ from the ____ node. This impulse spreads throughout the atria causing them to contract. This is known as _____ _____. Blood is now forced from the two atria into the two ventricles below. This stage of the cardiac cycle is known as _____ _____. During this stage the _____ valves are open but the _____ valves are closed. As the atria relax during _____ _____ they are filled with blood. As the cardiac impulse spreads throughout the ventricles, they contract causing _____ _____. Now the _____ valves are closed and blood is forced through the _____ valves into the aorta and the pulmonary arteries. Finally, the ventricles begin to relax, the _____ valves once again close whilst the _____ valves open. The ventricles once again fill with blood during _____ _____. The cycle now begins again.

7. Match the appropriate term to the correct definition of the dynamics of the heart.

- *Cardiac output*
- *Ejection fraction*
- *Stroke volume*
- *Frank-Starling's mechanism*
- *End-diastolic volume*

_____ A. The volume of blood that exists in the ventricles at the end of the relaxation or filling stage of the cardiac cycle.

_____ B. The volume of blood ejected by the heart per minute.

_____ C. The greater the stretch of the cardiac fibres, the greater the force of contraction which increases the stroke volume.

_____ D. The percentage of blood actually pumped out of the left ventricle per contraction.

_____ E. The volume of blood pumped out of the heart per beat.

8. Complete the table below taking one value from each box (stroke volume, heart rate and cardiac output) to give typical cardiac output values for the subjects identified.

HEART RATE			CARDIAC OUTPUT			STROKE VOLUME	
202	72		32	22		180	85
180	60		5	5		70	110

	HR × SV = Q (cardiac output)
Untrained at rest	
Untrained during exercise	
Trained at rest	
Trained during exercise	

9. The table below shows the responses of heart rate to exercise that might occur during a 5K run.

a. Using the information in the table, sketch a graph to illustrate the heart rate response. NB: Time should be placed along the x-axis.

Time (mins)	–2	–1	0	1	2	4	6	8	10	15	20	21	22	23	24	25	30
HR bpm	72	76	80	115	125	140	145	145	145	145	150	125	110	105	105	100	75

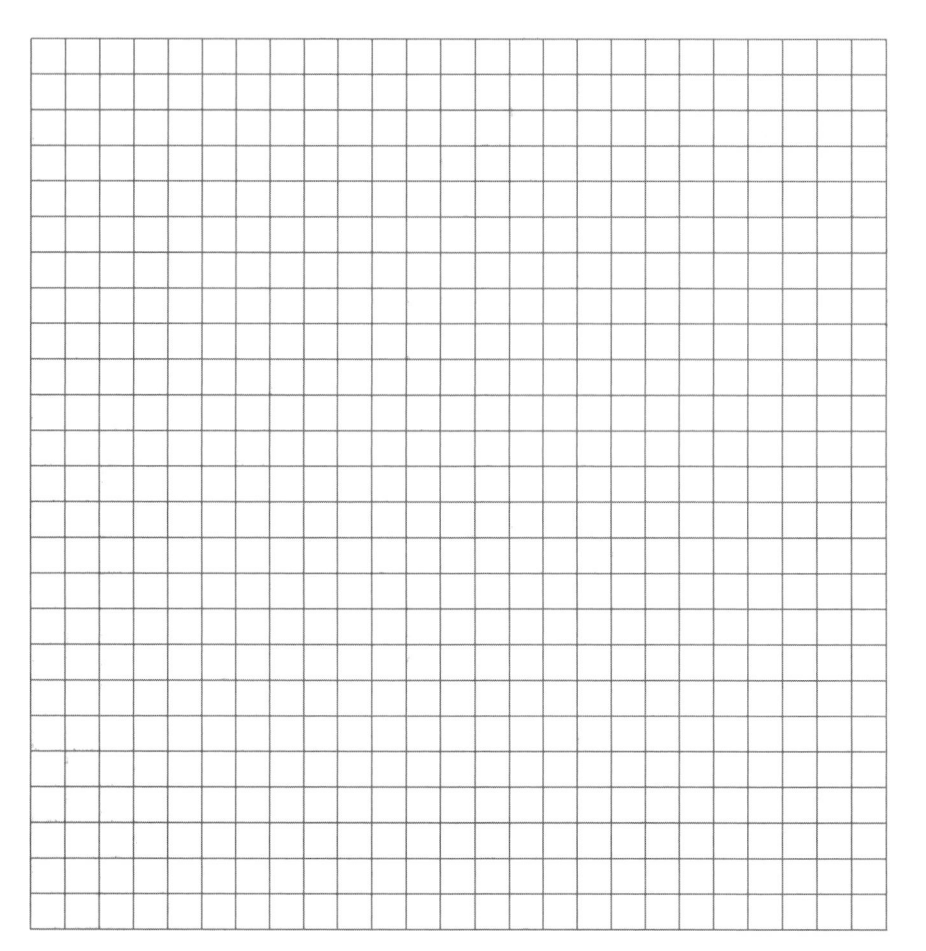

b. Explain the pattern of the heart rate curve, before, during and following the exercise.

Before: _____

_____

_____

During: _____

_____

Following: _____

_____

10. Fill in the missing gaps in the passage, choosing from the words given below. (You may use each word more than once.)

aorta	pocket valves	vein
arteries	pre-capillary sphincters	veins
arterioles	vasoconstruction	venae cavae
artery	vasodilation	venules
capillaries		

_____ carry blood away from the heart. The largest _____ in the body is the _____ . _____ get smaller and smaller the further we travel away from the heart. These smaller _____ are termed _____. They control the amount of blood flowing to the muscles through _____ and _____. _____ eventually feed into the _____, which are the smallest blood vessels. They have extremely thin walls which allows for the exchange of gases and helps provide essential nutrients to the working muscles. The flow of blood through the capillary bed is controlled by _____ _____. Blood leaves the capillary bed via small vessels called _____, which get larger and larger eventually forming _____. _____ possess _____ _____ which aids the flow of blood back to the heart. The largest _____ in the body is called the _____ _____.

11. Complete the table below with an explanation of how the structure of the vessel or mechanism identified suits its function.

	Structure	Function
Arteries/Arterioles		
Capillaries		
Pre-capillary sphincters		
Veins/Venules		
Pocket valves		
The muscle pump		

12. Below is a diagram of the double circulatory system. Label the parts of the diagram A–N, selecting the appropriate term from the list below. (You may use a term more than once.)

- Arteries
- Arterioles
- Pulmonary circulation system
- Systemic circulation system
- Capillaries in the lungs
- Capillaries in the muscles/tissues
- Venules
- Veins
- Right atrium
- Left atrium
- Right ventricle
- Left ventricle

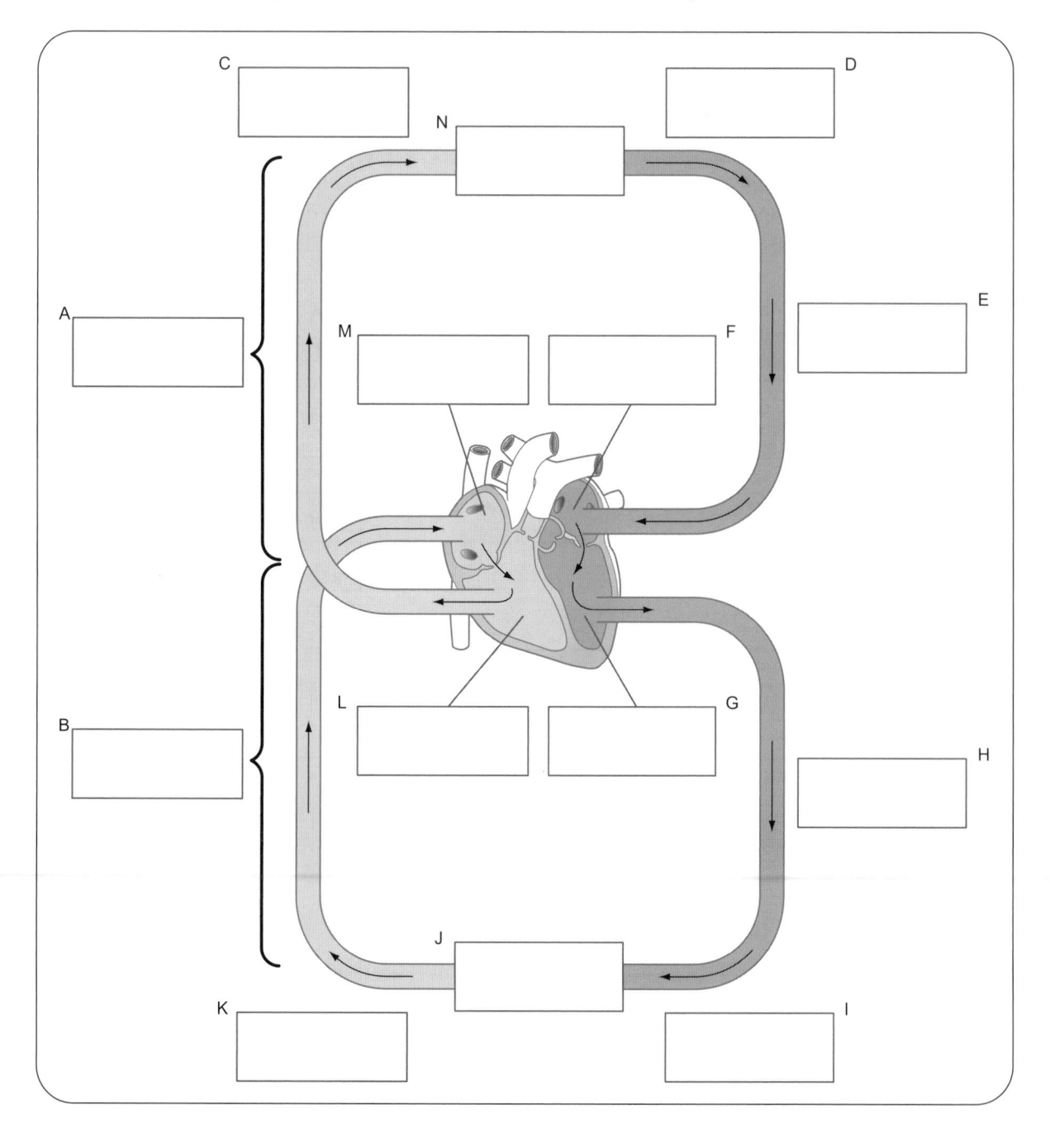

13. Match the following terms with the correct statement.

- *Aorta*
- *Arteries*
- *Arterioles*
- *Capillaries*
- *Veins*

_____ A. Vessels that together have the greatest cross-sectional area and the slowest velocity of blood flow through them.

_____ B. These vessels offer the lowest resistance to blood flow.

_____ C. At rest, the greatest volume of blood is contained in these vessels.

_____ D. These vessels offer the greatest resistance to blood flow.

_____ E. Blood flowing through this blood vessel has the highest velocity and the greatest pressure.

14. The graph below illustrates changes in blood pressure linked to blood vessel type.

On the same graph, draw the expected curve for:

a. Total cross-sectional area
b. Blood velocity

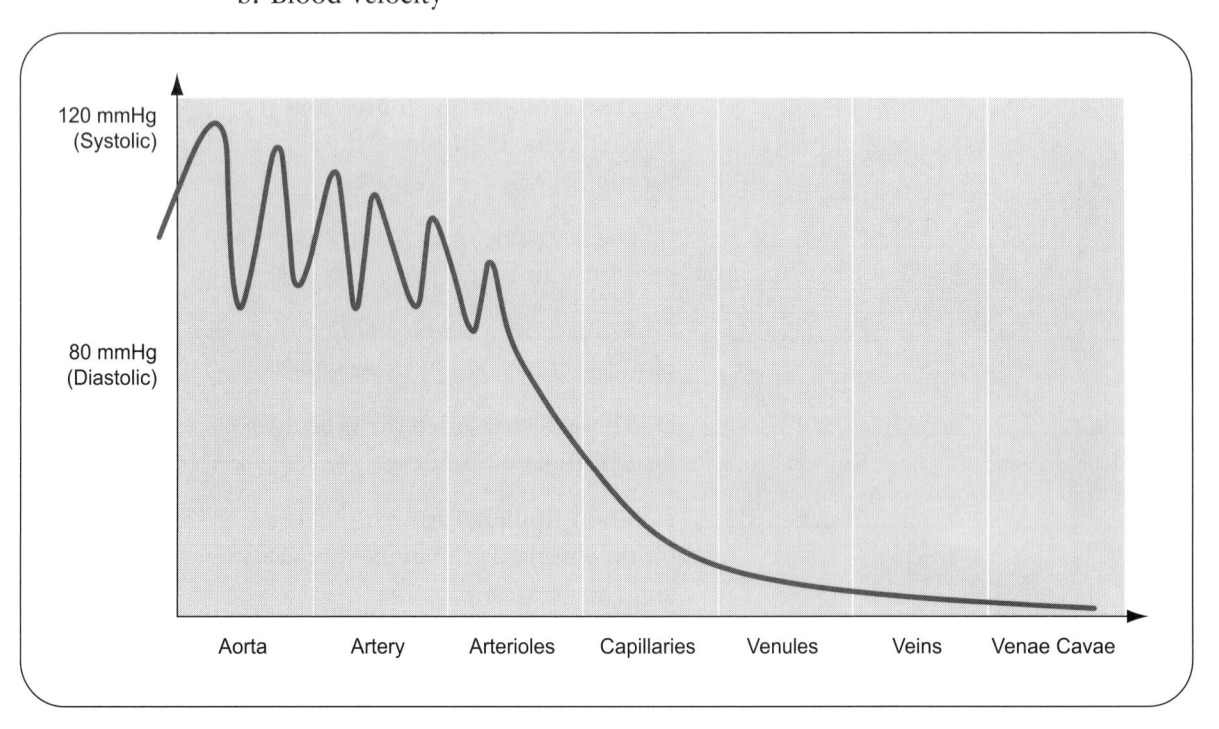

c. Briefly explain what happens to blood pressure during:

　i. An aerobic activity such as a 5K run.

_____

_____

_____

_____

_____

　ii. An anaerobic activity such as weight training.

_____

_____

_____

_____

_____

Chapter 3: The respiratory system – gaseous exchange and transport

1. Using the diagram of the respiratory system below, label the structures A–F.

- *Alveolar capillaries*
- *Bronchii*
- *Pleural cavity containing pleural fluid*
- *Alveolus*
- *Bronchiole*
- *Trachea*

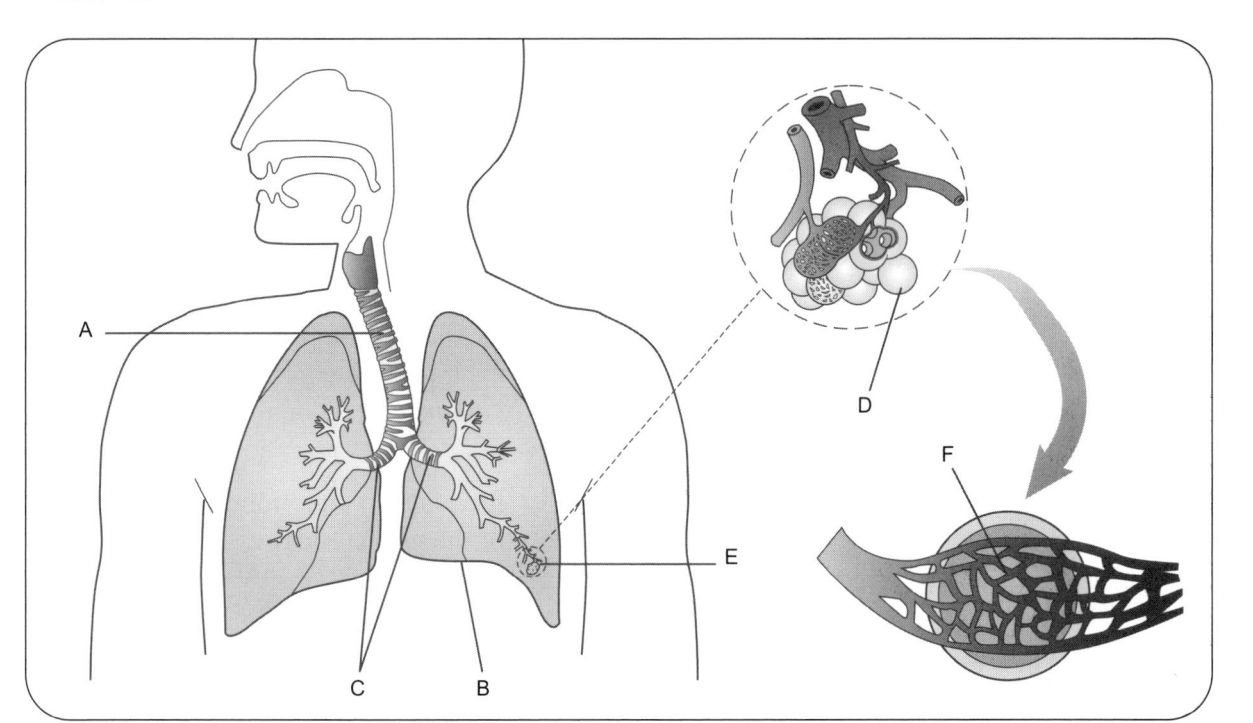

2. Match the following terms with the correct definition:

- *Internal intercostal muscles*
- *External intercostal muscles*
- *Diaphragm*

_____ A. Muscles of inspiration that move the rib cage upwards and outwards during inspiration.

_____ B. A large dome-shaped sheet of muscle that expands the thoracic cavity during inspiration.

_____ C. Muscles used for expiration during exercise.

3. Match the appropriate term to the correct definition of lung volumes and capacities.

- *Inspiratory reserve volume*
- *Expiratory reserve volume*
- *Tidal volume*
- *Total lung capacity*
- *Residual volume*
- *Vital capacity*

_____ A. The volume of air inspired or expired per breath during normal quiet breathing.

_____ B. The volume of air that remains in the lungs after maximal expiration.

_____ C. The volume of air that can be forcefully inspired following inspiration of the normal tidal volume.

_____ D. The maximal volume of air that can be forcefully expired after maximal inspiration.

_____ E. The sum of inspiratory and expiratory reserve volumes, tidal volume and residual volume.

_____ F. The volume of air that can be forcefully expired following expiration of the normal tidal volume.

4. Using the figure opposite and the numbers below, label the relative partial pressures of oxygen and carbon dioxide at sites A–E.

- *105mmHg*
- *0.3mmHg*
- *45mmHg*
- *40mmHg*
- *160mmHg*

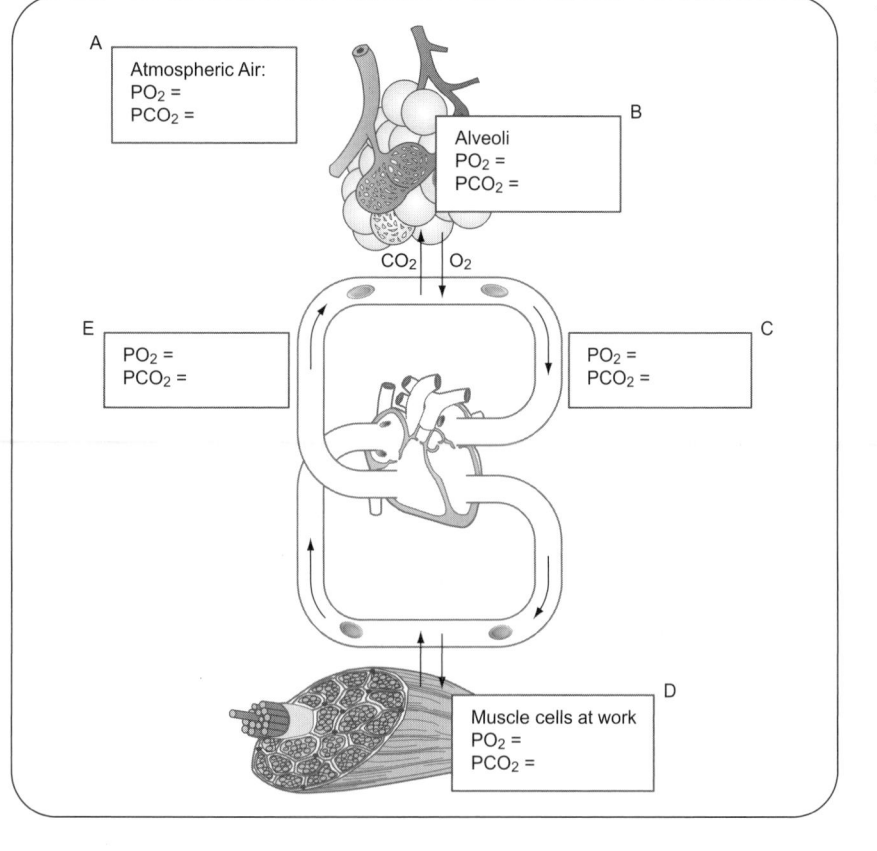

A Atmospheric Air:
PO_2 =
PCO_2 =

B Alveoli
PO_2 =
PCO_2 =

CO_2 O_2

E PO_2 =
PCO_2 =

C PO_2 =
PCO_2 =

D Muscle cells at work
PO_2 =
PCO_2 =

5. a. Study the data in the table below showing the percentage saturation of haemoglobin with oxygen at various partial pressures of oxygen. Now plot the data using a fairly large scale. Ensure that you have percentage (%) saturation of haemoglobin with oxygen on the y-axis and oxygen partial pressure (PO$_2$) on the x-axis.

% saturation of haemoglobin with oxygen	Partial pressure of oxygen (mmHg)
0	0
10	10
20	16
30	22
40	25
50	27
60	30
70	33
80	45
90	60
97	100

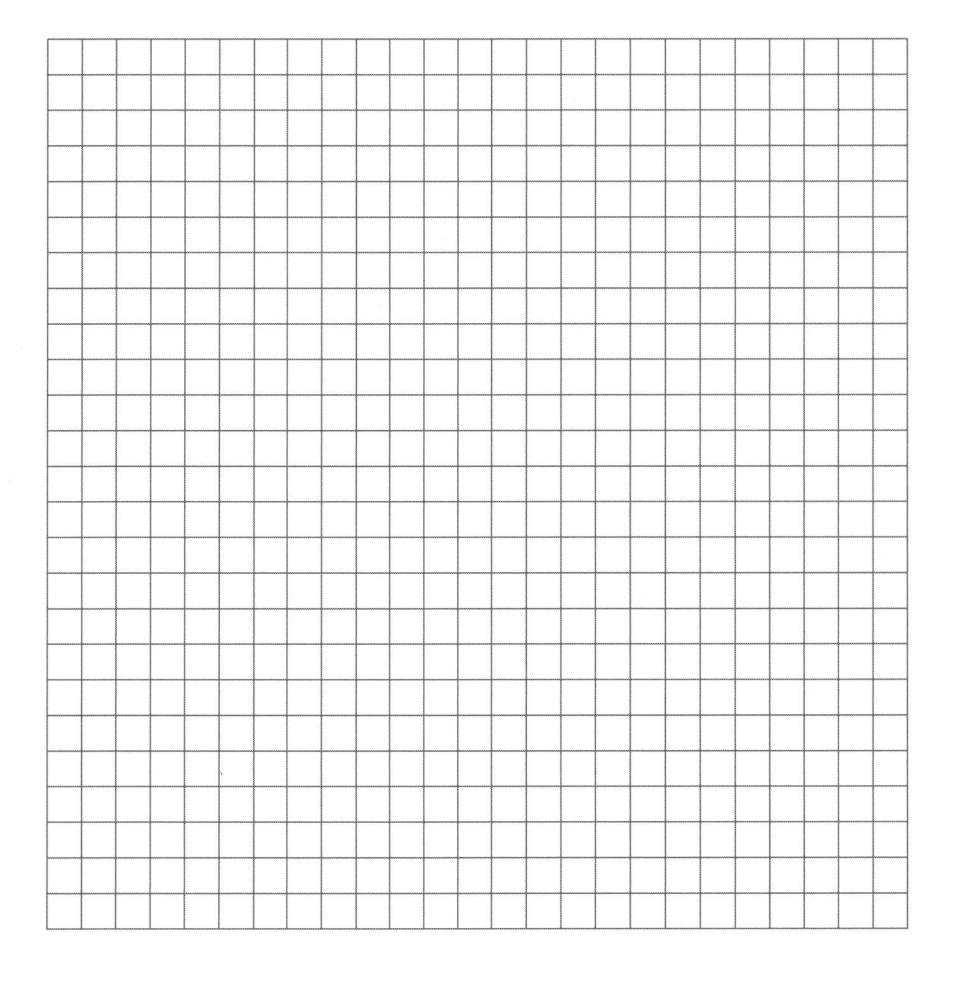

b. On the y-axis, find the point where haemoglobin is 50 per cent saturated with oxygen. Follow this line across to where it intersects the curve you have just plotted. Write down the corresponding PO$_2$ at 50 per cent saturation.

_____ mmHg

c. On your graph, sketch and label the corresponding dissociation curve for myoglobin. Briefly explain the positioning of your curve.

_____

_____

_____

_____

d. On your graph, sketch the curve that you might expect to see during exercise. Explain why this new curve may be beneficial to the athlete.

_____

_____

_____

_____

6. Fill in the missing gaps in the passage, choosing from the words given below.

low	oxygen	high
diffusion	partial pressure	carbon dioxide

Gases in the respiratory system move from areas of _____ pressure to areas of _____ pressure by the process of _____. It is in fact the _____ _____ of each gas that provides the driving force for this movement. In the alveoli the partial pressure of _____ is highest, whilst in the deoxygenated blood returning to the lungs it is the partial pressure of _____ _____ that is greatest.

7. Match the appropriate term to the correct statement.

- *Bohr effect*
- *Shift to the right*
- *Shift to the left*
- *Oxy-haemoglobin*
- *Decreases*
- *Increases*

_____ A. Haemoglobin molecule that has been saturated with oxygen.

_____ B. The movement of the oxy-haemoglobin dissociation curve due to an increase in carbon dioxide and blood temperature.

_____ C. The effect on haemoglobin saturation with oxygen resulting from increased blood acidity (low pH).

_____ D. The amount of oxygen bound to haemoglobin does this when the partial pressure of carbon dioxide increases.

Chapter 4: Defining and evaluating fitness

1. Using the diagram below, label all the components of fitness you are required to learn for your examination.

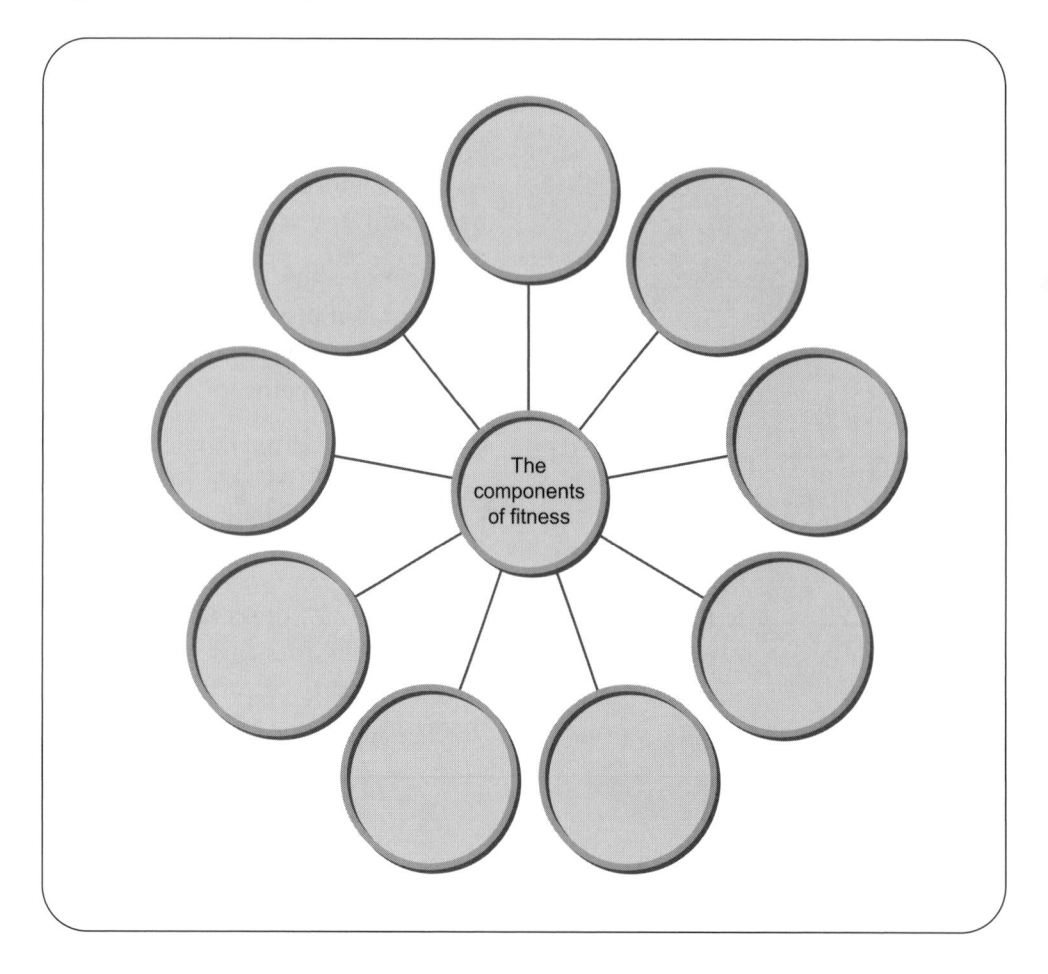

The components of fitness

2. Match the following terms to the correct definition.

- *Maximum strength*
- *Elastic strength*
- *Strength endurance*

_____ A. The ability to overcome a resistance rapidly and prepare the muscle quickly for a sequential contraction of equal force.

_____ B. The ability of a muscle or group of muscles to undergo repeated contractions and withstand fatigue.

_____ C. The maximum force that can be developed in a muscle or group of muscles during a single maximal contraction.

3. Match the appropriate term to the correct definition of the components of fitness. (You can use the terms more than once.)

- *Speed*
- *Balance*
- *Cardio-respiratory endurance*

- *Body composition*
- *Flexibility*
- *Agility*

_____ A. The relative components of total body mass in terms of fat mass and lean body or fat free mass.

_____ B. The ability to move and change the direction and position of the body quickly while maintaining good body control and without loss of speed.

_____ C. The maximum rate that a person can move over a specific distance.

_____ D. The range of movement possible at a joint.

_____ E. The maintenance of the body's centre of mass over the base of support.

_____ F. The ability to put body parts into motion quickly.

4. For each of the performers given, suggest the most appropriate fitness test from the list below.

- *PWC170 test*
- *Handgrip dynamometer test*
- *Multi-stage fitness test*
- *30m sprint test*

- *One rep. max. test*
- *Sit and reach test*
- *Vertical jump test*
- *Wingate cycle test*

_____ A. A test of power for a line out jumper in rugby.

_____ B. A test of cardio-respiratory endurance for a cyclist.

_____ C. A test of flexibility for a rower.

_____ D. A test of strength for a weightlifter.

_____ E. A test of cardio-respiratory endurance for a cross-country runner.

5. A subject performs the PWC170 test. Study the data in the table below.

Workload	Power output (Watts)	Heart rate (bpm)
1	120	118
2	150	135
3	180	156

a. Plot a graph with heart rate along the y-axis (vertical) and power output along the x-axis (horizontal) for each of the three workloads.

b. Draw a line of best fit through the three points and extend this line to a heart rate of 170 bpm. Read off the projected power output in Watts and write it in the space below.

Power output 170 bpm = _____

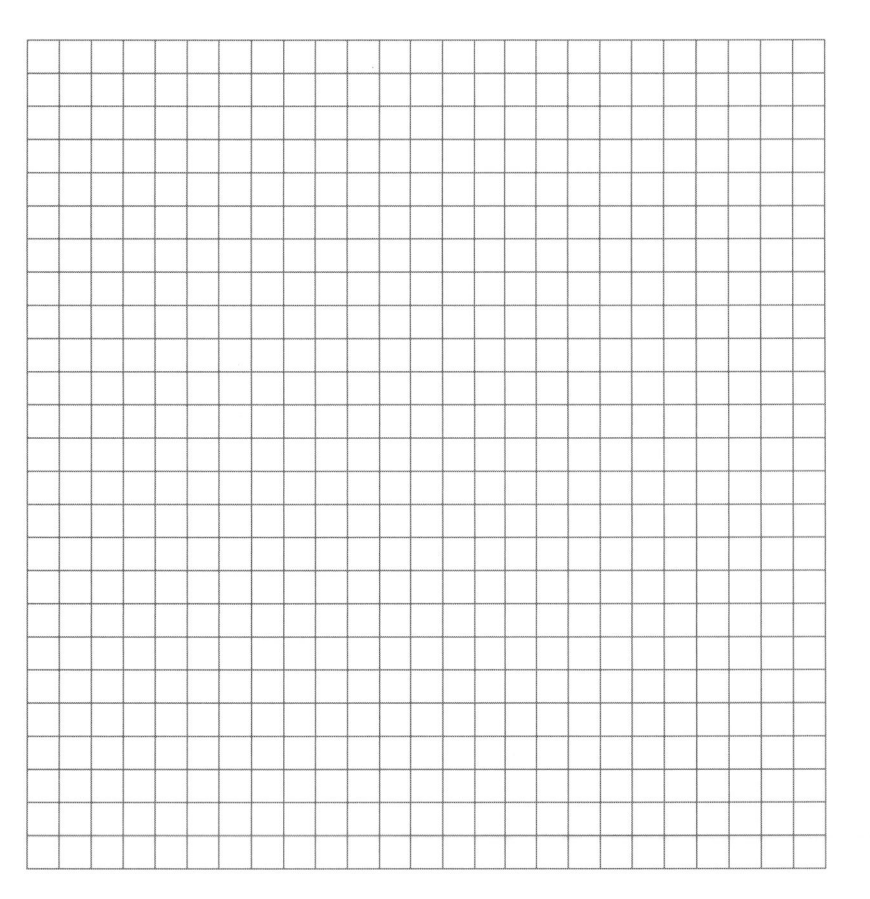

c. Briefly outline the strengths and limitations of this sub-maximal test as a test of aerobic capacity.

_____

_____

_____

_____

_____

6. Fill in the missing gaps of the passage, choosing from the words given below.

| reliability | maximal test | sub-maximal test | specific |
| testing environment | validity | practicality |

The _____ of fitness testing is concerned with whether a test actually measures what it claims to measure. If a test is _____, it will improve its _____. This can be achieved by ensuring the _____ _____ mimics the sporting situation. A measure of a fitness test's _____ is if the test results can be repeated when it is conducted a second or subsequent time (assuming that there has been no change in fitness levels). _____ tests tend to be more reliable than _____ tests as the motivation of the performer to work to exhaustion does not become a determining factor.

7. a. How might a gymnast apply the two dimensions of balance in a gymnastics competition?

_____

_____

_____

_____

_____

b. Explain, using examples, why the Illinois agility run test may be of more value to a rugby player than a 30m sprint test.

_____

_____

_____

_____

_____

c. Give an example of when a gymnast might require each of the three dimensions of strength.

_____

_____

_____

_____

_____

8. Now it's time to perform some fitness tests! Where possible, carry out the battery of fitness tests outlined below. Then complete the accompanying table, filling in your score.

Component of fitness	Recognised test	My score	My rating
Cardio-respiratory endurance (aerobic capacity)	Multi-stage fitness test	Level: Shuttle: VO$_2$max:	
Maximal strength	1. Handgrip dynamometer 2. One rep. max. test		
Strength endurance (muscular endurance)	Abdominal conditional test		
Elastic strength (power)	1. Wingate cycle test 2. Vertical (Sargent) jump test		
Speed	30m sprint test		
Flexibility	Sit and reach test		
Body composition	1. Skinfold measures 2. Bioelectric Impedance		
Agility	Illinois agility run test		
Balance	The standing stork test		

9. From your fitness test ratings, complete a fitness profile using the 'fitness ring' below. You will first need to write the components of fitness around the circumference of the rings.

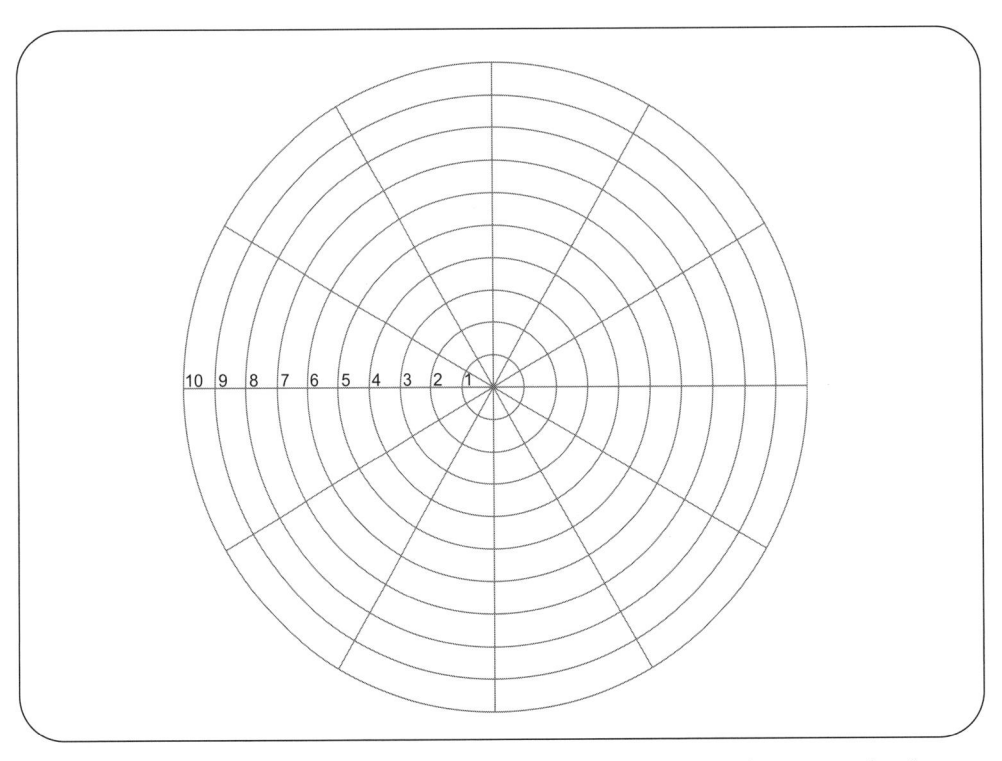

Now show the ideal fitness profile for an activity of your choice on the fitness ring below:

Activity: _____

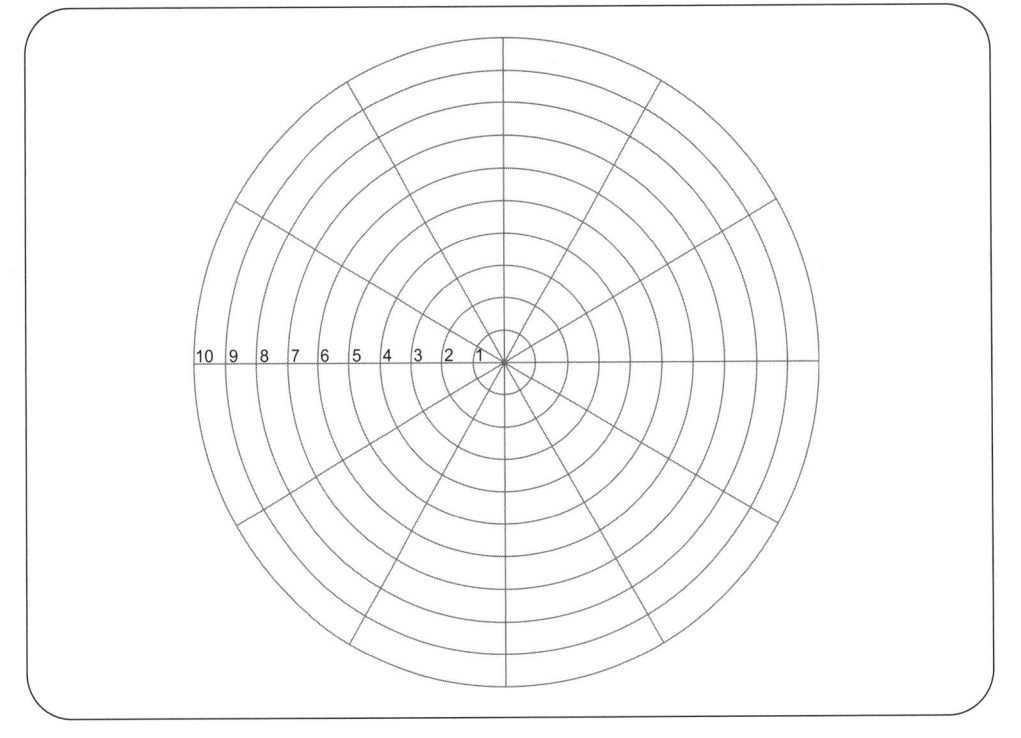

If you compare the two fitness rings, you can identify your strengths and weaknesses and devise an action plan to improve your performance!

Chapter 5: Defining the nature of skill and abilities

1. Complete the definition of skill using the words in the box below.

time	minimum outlay	energy
maximum certainty	pre-determined results	learned ability

Skill is the _____ _____ to bring about

_____ _____ with _____

_____, often with the _____ _____ of

_____ or _____ or both.

2. List five characteristics of a skilled performance.

a. _____

b. _____

c. _____

d. _____

e. _____

3. Outline the following types of skill. Use practical examples to illustrate your answers.

Type of skill	Explanation	Practical example
Cognitive skill		
Perceptual skill		
Motor skill		
Psychomotor skill		

4. For each of the skills listed below, construct a classification profile based on the continua outlined in the table. Work in pairs. Take turns to justify your reasons for the classification.

a Swimming stroke
b Triple jump
c Hockey penalty flick
d Netball set play
e Rugby line-out
f Basketball free-throw
g Golf swing
h Sprint start
i Cycling race
j Tennis serve

Classification of skill	a	b	c	d	e	f	g	h	i	j
Low										
High										
Simple										
Complex										
Open										
Closed										
Gross										
Fine										
Self-paced										
Externally-paced										
Discrete										
Serial										
Continuous										

5. Match up each of the statements in column A to the correct continua in column B.

A: Description	Answer	B: Classification
i. Skills involve performers initiating the start of the movement based on other people's actions, or changing events in the environment and the speed of the movement in relation to other people's actions, or changing events in the environment. Usually *open* skills.		a. Low
ii. Skills involve large muscle movements and large muscle groups. Accuracy and precision is not necessarily a high priority.		b. High
iii. Skills involve a linked series of discrete skills, performed in a set order or sequence for each subroutine.		c. Simple
iv. Skills are directly affected by the environment because it is unstable and changing; it is not predictable. Skills require constant adjustment to suit the situation. The skills are perceptual and involve decisions which need to be made quickly.		d. Complex
v. Skills involve: few subroutines; little information to process; time to evaluate the situation. Feedback would not be crucial during performance.		e. Open
vi. Skills involve subroutines which are difficult to separate and practise in isolation. The development of subroutines has usually to occur as part of the whole movement.		f. Closed
vii. Skills are not directly affected by the environment because it is stable and constant; it is predictable. The skills are pre-learned in a set routine, require minimal adjustment and can be repeated consistently when learnt. Decisions are pre-planned.		g. Gross
viii. Skills involve subroutines which are easily identified and separated from the movement. The subroutines can be practised in isolation and then developed as part of the whole movement.		h. Fine
ix. Skills involve a clear beginning and end, and take a short time for completion. To repeat the skill it must be started again.		i. Self-paced
x. Skills involve no clear beginning or end, and are performed over an extended time period. The end of one movement is the start of the next.		j. Externally-paced
xi. Skills involve small muscle movements and small muscle groups. Accuracy and precision is a vital factor.		k. Discrete
xii. Skills involve performers controlling the start and the speed of the movement. Usually *closed* skills.		l. Serial
xiii. Skills involve: numerous subroutines which need to be performed with the correct timing; a large amount of information to process; limited time to evaluate the situation. Feedback would be helpful during and after the performance.		m. Continuous

6. a. Explain the difference between skill and ability.

_____

_____

b. Outline the relationship between skill and ability.

_____

_____

7. For both of the activities below, list the four most important gross motor abilities and the four most important perceptual motor abilities required to produce a high level of performance. Justify your reasons for their inclusion.

a. Trampolining   b. Netball

Gross motor ability	Justification	Perceptual motor ability	Justification

Gross motor ability	Justification	Perceptual motor ability	Justification

Chapter 6: Learning and performance

1. Explain the difference between learning and performance.

_____

_____

_____

2. For each of the stages of learning listed below, outline their characteristics and the types of feedback most associated with each.

Stage of learning	Characteristics	Type of feedback
Cognitive		
Associative		
Autonomous		

3. The graph below represents a novice basketball player's attempts during a practice session to develop his shooting technique.

a. Identify each of the stages of learning highlighted by the letters A, B, and C.

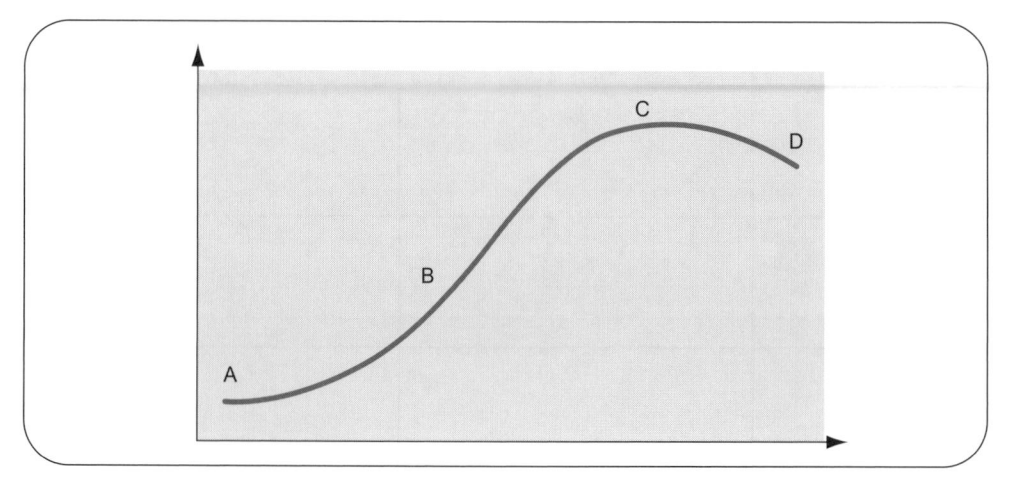

b. Suggest three possible causes of D and, for each, outline a suitable strategy to develop the level of performance further.

Possible cause	Strategy for improvement
i.	
ii.	
iii.	

4. Fill in the gaps using the words provided.

manipulating	error	reinforcement
behaviour	response	punishment
associationist theories	trial	stimulus

Operant conditioning is one of the _____ _____.
It involves the performer linking a specific _____ to a learned
_____. This is achieved by the coach _____ the
environment and providing either _____ or
_____, causing the S-R bond to be strengthened or
weakened. The aim is to shape _____ and the performer often
learns through _____ and _____.

5. Explain the following terms and give a practical example to illustrate your answer.

	Explanation	Example
Positive reinforcement		
Negative reinforcement		
Punishment		

6. Fill in the gaps using the words provided.

perception	whole	stimuli	thinking
understanding	responses	knowledge	

Cognitive theories of learning suggest an individual learns through _____ about and _____ what is required to solve the problem, rather than developing a series of _____ to various _____. The problem is solved as a _____, using previous _____ and _____.

7. List two advantages and two disadvantages of operant conditioning and the cognitive theories of learning.

Operant conditioning	Cognitive learning theories
Advantage 1:	Advantage 1:
Advantage 2:	Advantage 2:
Disadvantage 1:	Disadvantage 1:
Disadvantage 2:	Disadvantage 2:

8. Fill in the gaps using the words provided.

copying	cognitive	demonstration
competent	mental	vicarious
associative	observing	verbal

Social learning or observational learning theory suggests we learn by _____ others and then _____ their actions. This is known as a _____ experience. This usually occurs in the form of a _____ creating a clear _____ picture. It is particularly useful during the _____ and _____ stages of learning. In order to be effective the model must be _____ and _____ guidance should be used to highlight key points.

9. Bandura suggested observational learning occurred if four components were present. Explain each of the components listed below and illustrate your answer with a practical example.

	Explanation	Example
Attention		
Retention		
Motor reproduction		
Motivation		

10. Select a skill (for example, dribbling), and devise suitable practices, each based on one of the theories of learning below, to introduce it to a group of novice performers. Complete each practice with other students and evaluate the effectiveness of each.

Theory of learning	Evaluation
Operant conditioning	Advantages: Disadvantages:
Cognitive learning theories	Advantages: Disadvantages:
Observational learning	Advantages: Disadvantages:

Chapter 7: Optimizing learning and performance

1. On the diagram below, list three factors in each box that should be considered when planning a training session.

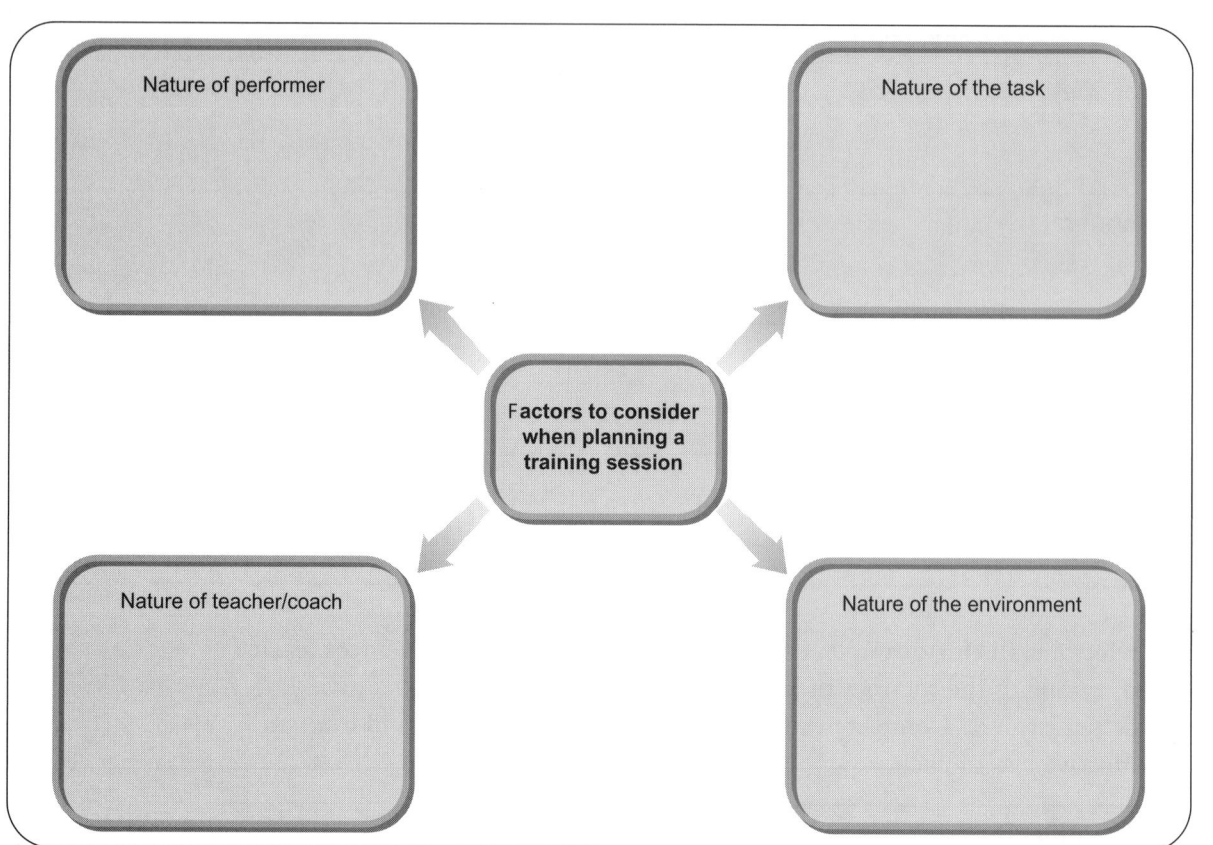

2. In the table below, for each form of *presentation of practice*, give a definition, two advantages, two disadvantages and an example of when each should ideally be used.

	Whole learning	Part learning
Definition		
Advantage 1		
Advantage 2		
Disadvantage 1		
Disadvantage 2		
Example		

3. Explain the terms *massed practice* and *distributed practice*.

_____

_____

_____

_____

_____

_____

4. Suggest four factors that would encourage the coach to use massed practice.

a. _____

b. _____

c. _____

d. _____

5. Suggest four factors that would encourage the coach to use distributed practice.

a. _____

b. _____

c. _____

d. _____

6. Fill in the gaps using the words provided.

mechanical	swimming float	video	verbal
dangerous	kinaesthetic	visual	demonstration
guidance	mental picture	manual	

The term _____ refers to information that is provided for the performer by the coach or teacher, allowing skills to be learnt more effectively. _____ guidance involves the performer creating a _____ _____ of the action. This can be achieved, for example, by _____ and _____. The coach can complement this form of guidance by highlighting relevant cues or providing feedback. This is known as _____ guidance. Another form of guidance involves the performer being physically moved, forced or supported into the correct position. This is usually referred to as _____ guidance and is useful when the situation may be _____ or require the performer to develop confidence, such as when learning a gymnastic vault. Finally, _____ guidance involves the performer being supported by some sort of device, for example, a _____ _____ or belt harness. The last two forms of guidance are used to develop the _____ awareness of a movement, developing timing and co-ordination.

7. Outline the forms of guidance you could use to introduce the skills listed below to a group of novice performers.

Justify your reasons and give practical examples to illustrate your answer.

• *Gymnastic vault*

_____

_____

_____

_____

_____

• *Swimming – front crawl*

_____

_____

_____

_____

_____

• *High jump*

_____

_____

_____

_____

_____

• *Set plays in a basketball game*

_____

_____

_____

_____

_____

• *Forehand tennis shot*

_____

_____

_____

_____

_____

8. Match each of the statements in column B to the correct teaching style in column A.

A		B
a. Command style		i. The teacher setting a problem and the learner devising a suitable solution. It is an open-ended approach, encouraging creativity whilst developing the cognitive and performance elements of the learner.
b. Reciprocal style		ii. The teacher guiding the learner to find the correct movement pattern by providing information, giving specific clues or asking questions when appropriate. The teacher acts as a facilitator
c. Discovery style		iii. The teacher making all the decisions with no input from the learners. An authoritarian manner is adopted by the teacher and all the performers complete the same actions.
d. Problem-solving style		iv. Most of the decisions being made by the teacher with some learner input. The task may be set by the teacher and be completed by the learners working in pairs, alternating the roles of performer and observer/coach.

9. Outline the teaching style you would adopt in the following situations and justify your reasons.

Novice performers throwing the javelin	
Novice performers developing gymnastic sequences	
Experienced basketball players developing their free throw technique during a team practice	

10. Explain the following terms and give two examples of each.

Intrinsic motivation: _____

_____

_____

Extrinsic motivation: _____

_____

_____

11. Which form of motivation is regarded as the most important to encourage participation, and why?

_____

_____

_____

_____

12. Complete the table below by indicating whether the examples are intrinsic (**I**) or extrinsic (**E**) forms of motivation.

Being awarded a personal swimming survival badge.		A professional receiving a monetary bonus for winning a match.	
Performing a somersault for the first time.		Being asked for a TV interview after the match.	
Reaching the top of a mountain.		Scoring a goal in a cup final.	
Receiving congratulations from another player after the game.		Setting a personal best.	
Being elected captain of a team.		Receiving a gold medal.	
Reading a report about yourself in the paper.		The teacher saying 'well done' during a lesson.	

13. Suggest four motivational strategies used by teachers or coaches to increase participation.

a. _____

b. _____

c. _____

d. _____

Chapter 8: Information processing

1. Label the information processing model shown below and explain each section with reference to a named sports skill.

Named skill: _____

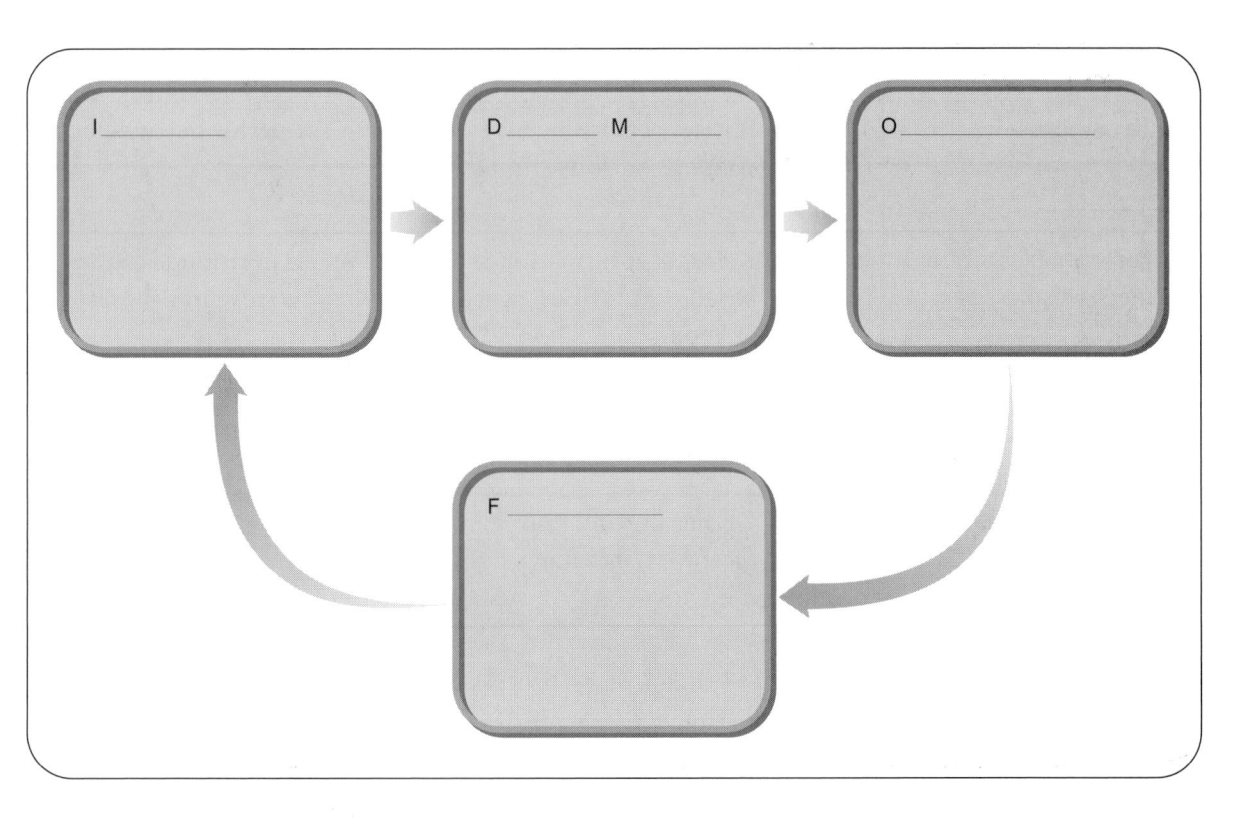

2. Explain what happens during the following phases of information processing.

Stimulus identification: _____

_____

_____

Response identification: _____

_____

_____

Response programming: _____

_____

_____

3. Match the words in column A below to the descriptions provided in column B.

A		B
a. Display		i. Interprets the gathered information and selects those stimuli which are relevant to the decision-making process.
b. Receptors		ii. Physical environment surrounding the performer which contains various stimuli.
c. Perceptual mechanism		iii. Relevant information is assessed and a decision is made based on previous experience, which is stored in the memory.
d. Translatory mechanism		iv. Selected motor programme or scheme is sent via the body's nervous system to the muscular system, allowing movement to occur.
e. Effector mechanism		v. Gather information from the environment using various receptors, including sight, sound, touch and smell. They are known as proprioceptors, exteroceptors, introceptors.

4. On the diagram of the memory process below, place the appropriate words listed in the correct sequence.

- *Long-term memory (LTM)*
- *Short-term sensory store (STSS)*
- *Input/Stimuli*
- *Recall*
- *Imagery*
- *Short-term memory (STM)*
- *Selective attention (SA)*
- *Encoding*
- *Recognition*
- *Motor programme*

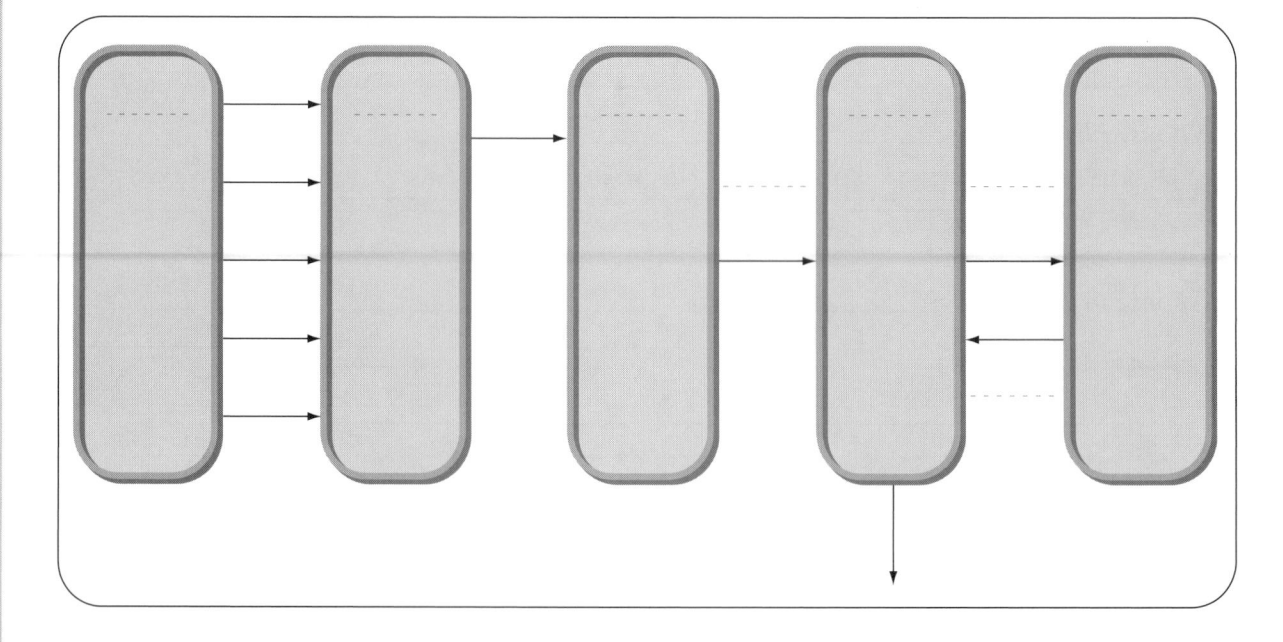

5. Outline the characteristics and function of each of the terms listed below.

Short-term sensory store	
Selective attention	
Short-term/ working memory	
Long-term memory	

6. Suggest three methods a performer could use to improve his or her long-term memory.

a. _____

b. _____

c. _____

7. Explain the following terms.

Reaction time: _____

_____

Movement time: _____

_____

Response time: _____

_____

8. Complete the diagram below using the terms listed, which is based on a sprint race.

- *Reaction time (A)*
- *Finish of race (D)*
- *Response time (B)*
- *Start of race (E)*
- *Movement time (C)*
- *Sound of gun (F)*

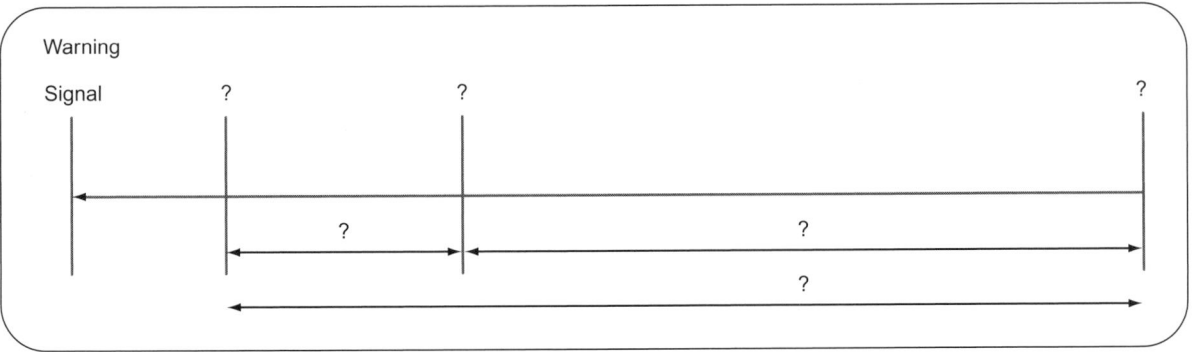

9. What is the difference between *simple reaction time* and *choice reaction time*?

_____

_____

_____

_____

_____

10. During a game a player successfully dummies an opponent, slowing her reaction time. Label the diagram below of the psychological refractory period.

- *Initial move to pass the ball (S1)*
- *Dummy move (S2)*
- *Initial reaction to intercept pass (R1)*
- *Reaction after dummy pass made (R2)*

11. List six factors that may affect your reaction time as a performer.

i. _____   iv. _____

ii. _____   v. _____

iii. _____   vi. _____

12. Outline three strategies that may improve your reaction time.

Strategy 1:
Strategy 2:
Strategy 3:

13. List three functions of feedback.

i. _____

ii. _____

iii. _____

14. Match the words in column A below to the descriptions provided in column B.

A		B	
a. Intrinsic feedback		i.	Used as a form of reinforcement, encouraging the performer to repeat the action.
b. Extrinsic feedback		ii.	Received during the performance via the proprioceptors and exteroceptors.
c. Continuous feedback		iii.	Information that the performer receives about the quality of his or her technique or performance.
d. Terminal feedback		iv.	Received from outside the performer, usually via sound or vision via their exteroceptors. The information is given by a coach, teacher, supporters, team mates, video or photographs.
e. Positive feedback		v.	Information concerning the outcome of the action. It may be the number of goals scored, recorded times and distances, or the statistics collected concerning accuracy and completed shots or passes.
f. Negative feedback		vi.	Received after the performance has been completed.
g. Knowledge of results		vii.	Used if the technique was incorrect, to discourage a repetition of the action.
h. Knowledge of performance		viii.	Received from within the performer via proprioceptors, and known as kinaesthetic feedback. As the performer becomes more skilled he or she is able to detect and correct his or her own errors more easily.

15. Outline six factors that would make the use of feedback more effective.

i. _____

ii. _____

iii. _____

iv. _____

v. _____

vi. _____

Chapter 9: Motor programmes and movement control

1. Explain the term *executive motor programme*.

_____

_____

_____

2. On the diagram below, for a named motor skill, break down the executive motor programme into its hierarchy of subroutines.

Refer to your chosen practical for the initial five phases of the skill.

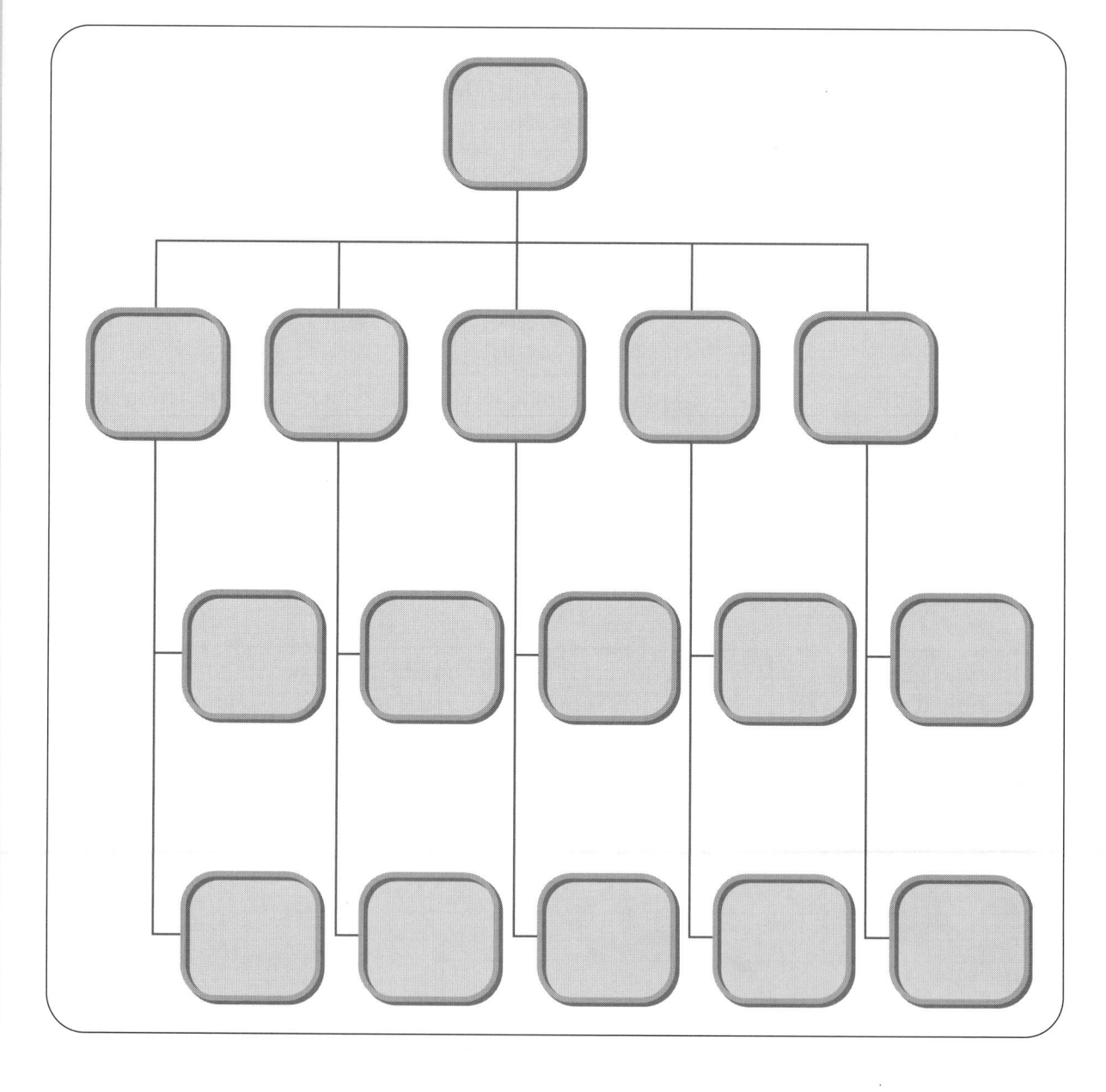

3. How can the executive motor programme be relegated to a subroutine and why is this desirable?

_____

_____

_____

_____

4. Suggest two weaknesses of the *motor programme theory*.

a. _____

_____

b. _____

_____

5. Fill in the gaps using the words provided.

open loop	perceptual	executive motor programme	subconscious
closed loop	modification	conscious	closed loop
comparison	feedback	long-term memory	feedback
memory	muscle spindles	kinaesthetic awareness	three

Once the _____ _____ _____ has been
selected the movement has to be regulated and adapted. It has been proposed
this occurs on _____ levels. Level 1 or _____ _____ control
suggests that some movements are performed without _____
control and appear automatic. Such movements are stored in the _____-
_____ _____, are retrieved very quickly when required and are
then completed without the need of _____. This is also known as the
_____ trace.

Level 2 or _____ _____ control involves some feedback
which is received via _____ _____ and the
_____ _____. Any errors are detected and adjustments
are made at a _____ level, with little direct attention from the
performer.

Level 3 is also _____ _____ control but involves a
conscious decision by the performer based on _____ received. The
performer has to pay attention to specific details and has to concentrate and
make a deliberate attempt to alter the movement pattern.

Levels 2 and 3 are also known as the _____ trace, allowing
_____ and _____ of movements when compared
to a stored model.

6. The table below shows a variety of activities. Indicate if you think the movement is under open or closed loop control.

Sporting situation	Level of control
Continuous chest pass	
Forward roll to balance	
Hockey push pass	
Walking along an upturned bench	
Running 200m in 40 seconds, with the aid of a stopwatch to monitor your time	
Dribbling a football between a series of cones	
Badminton rally	
Five basketball free throws	

7. Suggest two possible weaknesses of the open and closed loop theory of motor control.

a. _____

_____

b. _____

_____

8. Fill in the gaps using the words provided.

information   generalized   modified   movements   experiences

The schema theory suggests we have a _____ series of _____ based on previous _____ that can be _____ based on the _____ available to the performer.

9. Outline the main functions of:

Recall schema: _____

_____

_____

Recognition schema: _____

_____

_____

10. Complete the blanks in the boxes below to give specific examples of the sources of information received in each type of schema.

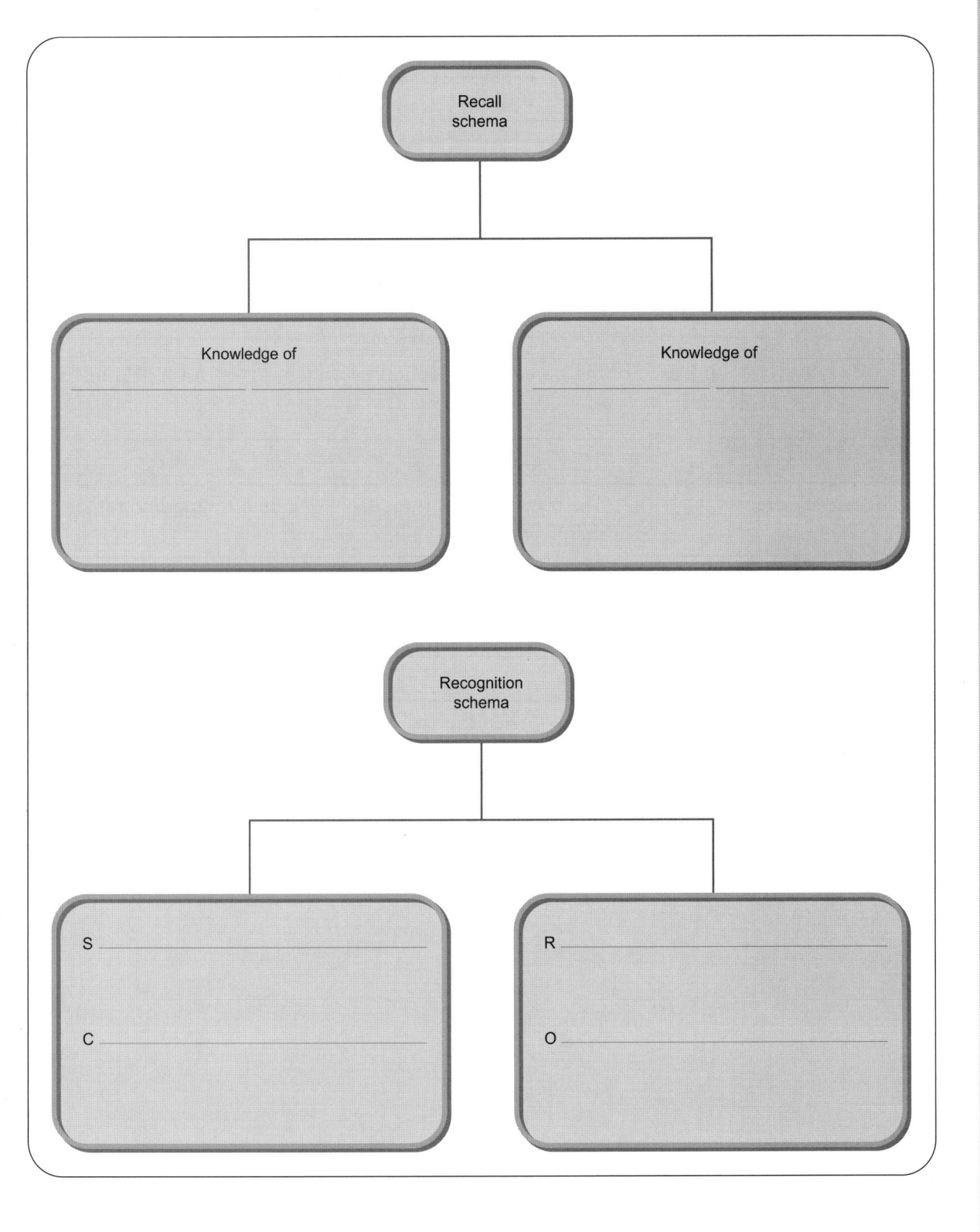

11. Suggest four ways in which a coach could ensure that strong schemas are developed.

a. _____

_____

b. _____

_____

c. _____

_____

d. _____

_____

12. Link each of the statements in column A to the correct form of transfer in column B.

A		B
a. Positive transfer		i. The transfer of learning from one limb to another, rather than from skill to skill.
b. Negative transfer		ii. Occurs when the skill being learnt has an effect on skills developed in the future.
c. Bilateral transfer		iii. When previously learnt skills help the development of new skills.
d. Proactive transfer		iv. Occurs when the skill being developed has an effect on one which has been previously learnt.
e. Retroactive transfer		v. When previously learnt skills hinder the development of new skills.

Unit 2: Socio-cultural and historical effects on participation in physical activity and their influence on performance

Chapter 10: The changing nature of British society

1. Fill in the table below listing as many characteristics as you can for popular recreation and rational recreation.

Popular recreation e.g. mob football	Rational recreation e.g. lawn tennis

2. How did the 'civilising of society' become reflected in recreation and sporting activities?

_____

_____

3. Suggest three ways in which popular recreation reflected the lifestyle of a peasant in pre-industrial Britain.

a. _____

b. _____

c. _____

4. What impact did the industrial revolution have on British society?

_____

_____

_____

_____

5. How did the industrial revolution initially restrict the recreational opportunities of the working classes and later improve them?

Initial restrictions	Later improvements

6. How and why did the Church encourage the new forms of rational recreation?

How? _____

_____

_____

Why? _____

_____

_____

7. In pre-industrial Britain there were two social classes: the lower and upper classes. How did the middle class emerge as a third social class and what was the legacy of the nineteenth-century middle classes on sport and society?

The middle classes emerged as a result of the i _____
r _____.

The legacy of the middle classes was:

Society: _____

_____

_____

Sport: _____

_____

_____

8. How did the role of women change in the early part of the twentieth century?

_____

_____

_____

_____

9. Public provision of recreational facilities, such as the provision of parks, began in the latter part of the nineteenth century and continues to the present day.

What were the motives for public provision?

a. _____

b. _____

c. _____

d. _____

10. What were the main features of Edwardian sport?

_____

_____

_____

_____

_____

_____

11. Match the words and phrases from column A to the appropriate sentences from column B.

A		B
a. Railways		i. This man was the headmaster of Rugby school featured in the book *Tom Brown's Schooldays* by Thomas Hughes.
b. Industrial patronage		ii. The development of towns as a result of the industrial revolution.
c. Dr Thomas Arnold		iii. They encouraged the popularity of the excursion, such as day trips to the seaside, as well as outdoor activities such as rambling and cycling.
d. British Empire		iv. The Cadbury factory in Birmingham was proactive in improving working conditions and general living standards for their workers.
e. Proprietary colleges		v. The middle classes had to build their own to educate their sons.
f. Urbanization		vi. It allowed the spread of sport across the world and into many different cultures.

12. This picture shows a **post-industrial game** of Association Football.

I know this because: _____

_____

_____

_____

_____

_____

_____

_____

_____

_____

_____

_____

_____

_____

_____

_____

_____

_____

_____

_____

Chapter 11: The development of physical education

1. State the *characteristics* of both public schools and state schools in the nineteenth century.

Public schools	State schools

2. Public schools became renowned for team games. How did public schools help in the *technical development* of team games?

_____

_____

_____

_____

_____

3. What *values* were associated with team games?

_____

_____

_____

_____

4. There were three stages in the development of public school athleticism.
Give a brief explanation of each phase.

- Phase 1 (bullying & brutality 1790–1828)

_____

_____

_____

- Phase 2 (Arnold & social control 1828–42)

_____

_____

_____

- Phase 3 (the cult of athleticism 1842–1914)

_____

_____

_____

5. Fill in the features of athleticism in the table below.

Physical endeavour	Moral integrity

6. What was the role of the sixth form in the development of games?

_____

_____

_____

7. How did the rational game of Association Football match the concept of athleticism? Write your answer using the table below.

Athleticism	Football

8. Complete the text below on physical education in state schools by filling in the gaps.

The watershed date for state school education was _____.

A form of gymnastics that relied on free flowing exercises was S_____
G _____.

The Model Course was established as a result of the B___ W___.

Military drill had three main aims:

a. _____

b. _____

c. _____

NCO stands for _____.

Military drill was abolished because it was un_____.

The S_____ of P_____ T_____ were published in 1904, 1909, 1919
and 1933.

After 1933 the teaching of physical education became d_____.

Moving and Growing *was a publication devised to provide guidelines for*
p_____ s_____.

Moving and Growing *focused on developing _____*

_____

_____

_____

_____

9. Fill in the table below and on the next page. Use the guidelines already completed for the first phase.

Date	Type of activity	Characteristics	Reasons	Problems
1870 Forster Education Act terms: State schools Elementary schools	Military Drill	War Office exercises Regimented/straight lines NCO & teachers Command–obey Dummy weapons Static/free-standing Boys first, girls later No age distinctions Compulsory/centralized Working-class kids not required to think/class response No interaction	To train working classes for: • military preparation • work preparation • discipline/obedience • fitness. Useful for: • accepting place in society • cheap/little space needed.	No education content Adult exercises for children Low status NCO
1890	Swedish Drill, included gymnastics			
1902–4	Model Course devised by Colonel Fox of War Office			
1904–19	Reinstatement of Swedish gymnastics First syllabus of PT Board of Education			
1914–18	First World War			

Date	Type of activity	Characteristics	Reasons	Problems
1933	Last of the syllabuses of PT			
1939–45	Second World War			
1952	*Moving and Growing* *Planning the* *programme*			
1950s–88	Decentralized			
1988 National Curriculum				

10. a. Why did the government establish a National Curriculum in 1988?

_____

_____

_____

_____

b. How did the National Curriculum improve the teaching of physical education and what are the possible restrictions of a national curriculum?

Improvements	Restrictions

c. What roles, other than a performer, does the National Curriculum encourage children to adopt?

_____

_____

_____

_____

Chapter 12: The administration and organization of sport in the UK

1. Write a brief explanation for each of the four levels shown in the performance pyramid below.

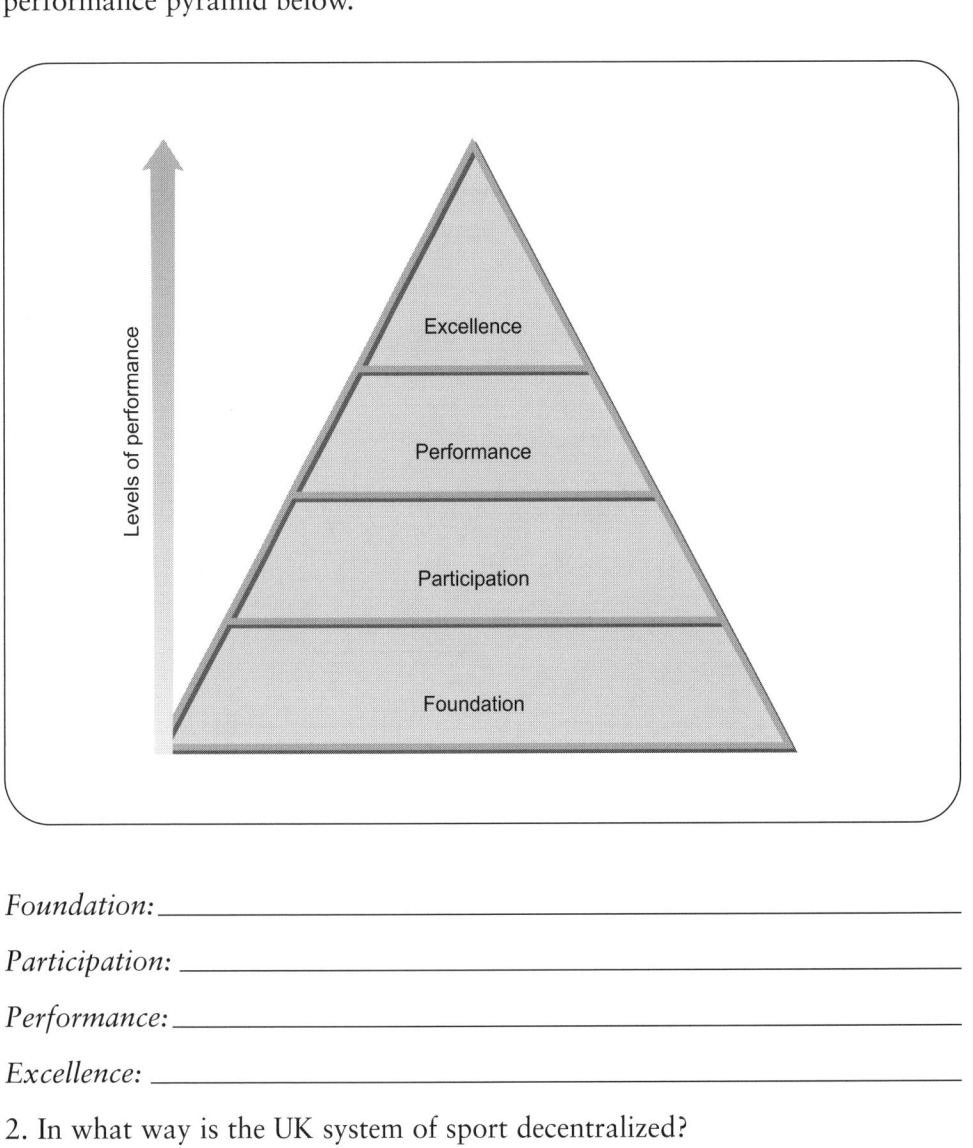

Foundation: _____

Participation: _____

Performance: _____

Excellence: _____

2. In what way is the UK system of sport decentralized?

_____

_____

_____

3. Name the four sectors responsible for the delivery of sport and active recreation in the UK.

a. _____

b. _____

c. _____

d. _____

4. What do the following abbreviations stand for?

DCMS _____

BST _____

NGB _____

LA _____

YST _____

5. Local authorities do not by law have to provide recreation and sporting facilities for their local community. Why should they choose to do so?

_____

_____

_____

_____

6. Name the three major government policies for sport in the UK since the 1980s?

a. _____

b. _____

c. _____

7. Sport in the UK receives significant funding from the National Lottery. Discuss the advantages and disadvantages of lottery funding for sport.

Advantages	Disadvantages

8. Give nine reasons for government involvement in sport.

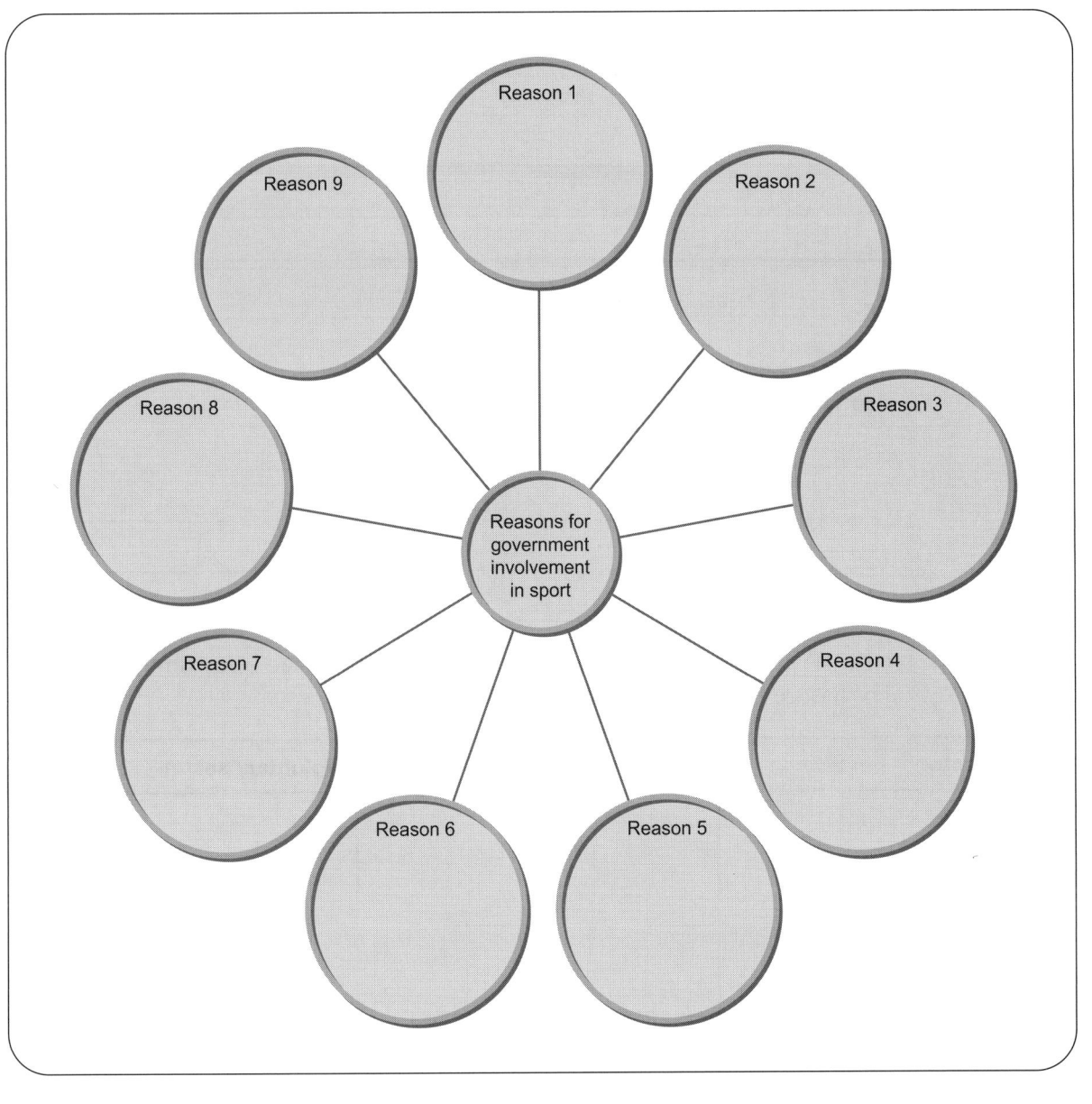

9. 'Best value' is a key government policy. What are its aims?

_____

_____

_____

_____

_____

_____

_____

10. What impact does sport have on a local community?

a. _____

b. _____

c. _____

d. _____

e. _____

f. _____

g. _____

h. _____

11. Regeneration is:

_____

_____

_____

_____

12. Write down the characteristics of each sector listed below in its provision of leisure for a local community.

Public sector	Private sector	Voluntary sector

13. The four objectives of Sport England are:

a. _____

b. _____

c. _____

d. _____

14. Complete in the following table.

Organization	Aims: What an organization is trying to achieve/its mission or purpose	Policies: The strategy or action plan put in place to achieve the aims
DCMS		
Sport England		
Sport Leaders UK (formerly British Sports Trust)		
Local authorities		

Chapter 13: Equal opportunities in the participation of physical recreation and sport

1. Stratification is the division of society into layers based on the following criteria:

a. Give examples for each. An example would be 'age' under biological.

- *biological:*_____

- *economic:* _____

- *social*: _____

The *dominant group* controls the more subordinate groups and the major social institutions, for example, education, politics, health, religion, media and so on. The dominant group has greater access to scarce resources and the power to control the distribution of resources.

In the UK the dominant group would be white, male, middle class and able bodied.

b. Who would the subordinate groups be?

_____

_____

2. Discrimination means making a distinction or giving unfair treatment, especially because of prejudice. It occurs when opportunities available to one social group are not available to all, and when a prejudicial attitude is acted upon.

There are two types of discrimination: *overt discrimination* and *covert discrimination*.

a. Give some examples of each type of discrimination in the table below.

Term	Examples
Overt discrimination (open to view)	
Covert discrimination (attitudes are harder to see)	

b. When subordinate groups in society are discriminated against, their opportunities are limited, including opportunities of social mobility (the ability of individuals to move up or down the social ladder).

List the factors that can lead to discrimination in sport and an action plan that could help reduce those problems.

_____

_____

_____

_____

_____

_____

_____

_____

_____

_____

_____

_____

_____

_____

_____

3. The graph below shows the overall levels of participation in sport (at least one activity excluding walking) over a period of 4 weeks and how this compares with the national average.

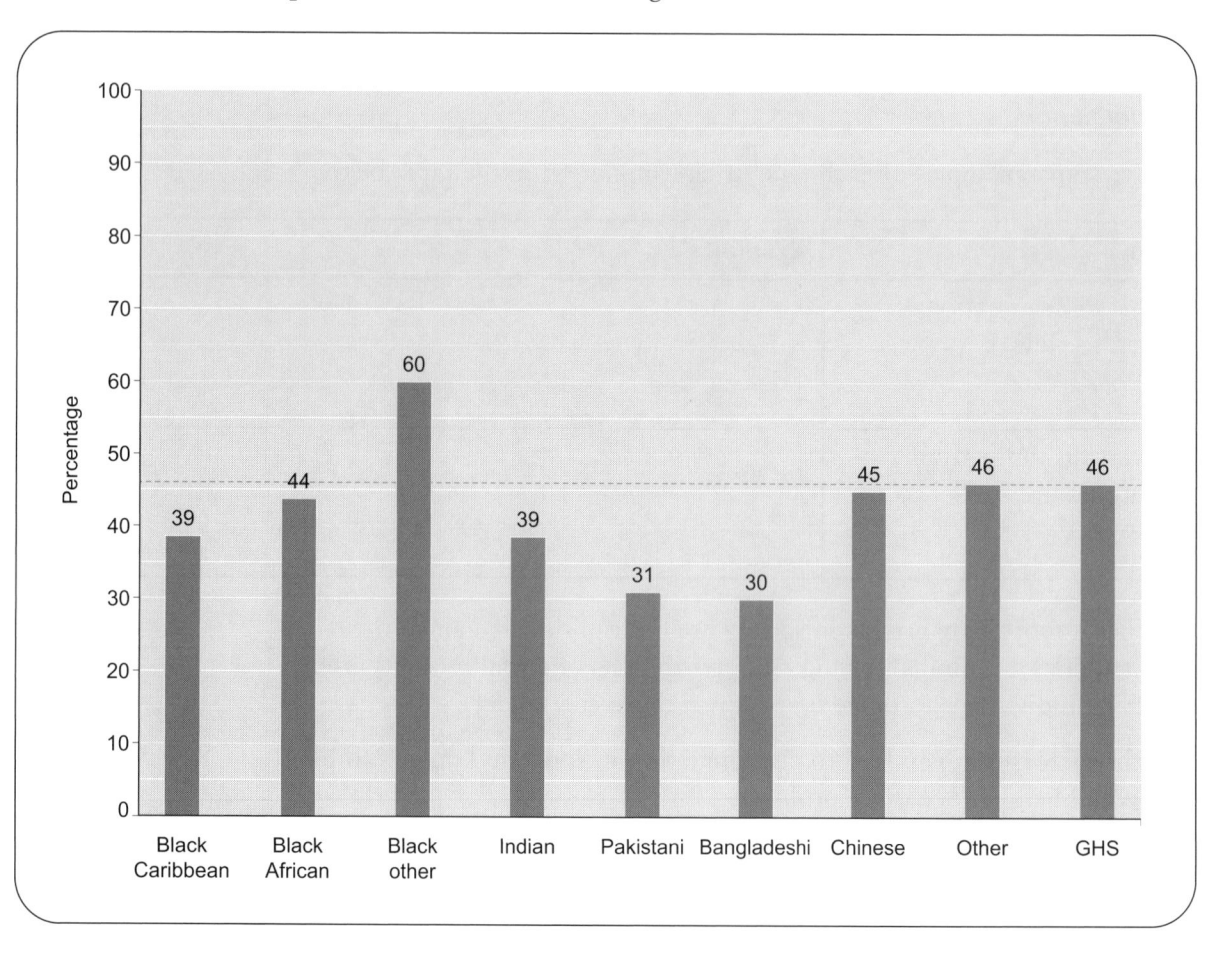

Account for the difference in the participation rates between ethnic minority groups (40 per cent) and the national average (46 per cent).

_____

_____

_____

_____

_____

_____

_____

_____

4. You need to understand the equity issues for the following social groups: low socio-economic (including low-income households, single-parent families and the unemployed), ethnic minorities, women and the disabled.

Look at the two tables that follow for women and ethnic minority groups. Complete similar tables for the other two groups (low socio-economic and the disabled). You could complete this task in groups or as a whole class.

Women

Characteristics	Problems of participation	Benefits of participation	Strategies to increase participation	Organizations involved
housewives	Lack of:	fitness	childcare provision	local authorities
mothers	• time	health	publicity leaflets	Physical Education
single	• transport	socialising	media coverage	local clubs
working	• confidence	confidence	female only sessions	governing bodies
unemployed	• experience	discount off-peak times	female leaders/coaches	Sport England
young	• childcare.		more competitions	Women's Sport Foundation
retired	media coverage		financial support at higher levels	Youth Sport Trust
ethnic group	role models			
	financial support			
	stereotypes			
	femininity v. sport roles			
	sexism			

Ethnic minority groups

Characteristics	Problems of participation	Benefits of participation	Strategies to increase participation	Organizations involved
Different: • races • nationalities • religions • attitudes towards sport.	racism isolation different values/attitudes finance stereotypes/expectations lack of role models co-educational classes at school sporting traditions different to facility provision in UK	health fitness socializing integration	sport activity promoters understand cultural issues publicity material in different languages leaders/coaches from community anti-racist approach segregated transport and sessions for women increased media coverage	Commission for Racial Equality Sport England demonstration projects local authorities

Low socio-economic

Characteristics	Problems of participation	Benefits of participation	Strategies to increase participation	Organizations involved

Disabled

Characteristics	Problems of participation	Benefits of participation	Strategies to increase participation	Organizations involved

Chapter 14: Exploring the different concepts of physical performance

1. Use the following columns to summarize the key points of the concepts of play, leisure, recreation, physical education and school sport, outdoor and adventurous activities, and sport. Use the template provided on play as a guideline.

Remember to learn the key points for each! The importance of this task is to use the key points to answer examination-style questions. It should also help you to cross-reference across each concept.

PLAY	LEISURE	RECREATION	PHYSICAL EDUCATION	OUTDOOR ACTIVITIES	SPORT
Definition: 'Play is a voluntary activity or occupation exercised within certain fixed rules of time and space, according to rules freely accepted and absolutely binding, having its aim in itself and accompanied by a feeling of tension, joy, and the consciousness that this is different from ordinary life.' [Huizinga] *Characteristics:* **spontaneous** because: no set rules/ boundaries/ time; **creative/expressive** because: children make up and change rules/ games/activities; **developmental/ experiential** learning **skills**/motor; perceptual; social & emotional **intrinsic**/fun/enjoyable **autonomy** because children officiate themselves Contd					

PLAY	LEISURE	RECREATION	PHYSICAL EDUCATION	OUTDOOR ACTIVITIES	SPORT
initiative decision making/negotiation **voluntary choice non-serious** (end product) **children master reality** through **role rehearsal/mimicry/ pretence** repetitive/ familiarity/security **socializing/play group**/flexible **social skills/** interaction **wholly absorbed** in activity **adults step away from reality** through relaxation/ catharsis					
Constraints on children's play: **Time:** break/falling out/boredom. **Space:** playground/ garden/share with others. **Safety:** imposed limits/equipment.					
Benefit to society: socialization (learning of cultural values, e.g. respect others; obey rules); integration; socializing; traditions passed down/ continuity					

2. State at least four factors that have resulted in a growth in leisure time for the majority of the population.

_____

_____

_____

_____

3. What are the similarities and differences between physical recreation and play?

Similarities:

_____

_____

_____

Differences:

_____

_____

_____

4. Name four aims of physical education.

a. _____

b. _____

c. _____

d. _____

5. What is the conceptual difference between physical education and sport?

Physical education	Sport

6. What is the difference between real and perceived risk?

Real risk is: _____

_____

Perceived risk is: _____

_____

7. Explain the highlighted words in the following definition of sport:

'*institutionalized competitive* activities that involve vigorous *physical exertion* or the use of relatively complex physical skills whose participation is motivated by a combination of *intrinsic and extrinsic* factors'.

- *institutionalized:* _____

- *competitive:* _____

- *physical exertion:* _____

- *intrinsic and extrinsic:* _____

_____

8. What are the benefits and problems that can be associated with sport for society?

Benefits of sport to society	Problems of sport for society

9. Sporting activities can be classified into categories. Explain the terms for these categories: *athletic*, *game* and *gymnastic*.

Category of activity	Explanation
athletic	
game	
gymnastic	

Mark scheme

1. a. 1 Triceps;
    2 Concentric/isotonic;
    3 Extension/flexion to extension. **(3 marks)**

1. b. 1 1st class/order lever;
    2 Correct labels – effort/fulcrum/load or equivalent;
    3 Correct order – fulcrum/pivot/joint in the middle. **(3 marks)**

1. c. i. 1 Positive – when a stimulus increases the probability of a desired response;
    2 For example – success at a skill/praise from coach, etc.
    3 Negative – when the stimulus is withdrawn when the desired response occurs;
    4 For example – removal of noise from crowd at increasing success of visiting player;
    5 Punishment – giving a stimulus to prevent a response occurring;
    6 For example – being shouted at by coach/rest of team. **(6 marks)**

1. c. ii. 1 Trial and error learning;
    2 Successful response reinforces/associated with stimulus/strengthens S0-R bond;
    3 Shaping/altering environment to progress toward success;
    4 For example – use of rewards/praise to reinforce learning/performance. **(any three for 3 marks)**

Sample answer

1. a. *The main agonist muscle working at the elbow is the tricep brachii. The type of muscle contraction is an isotonic contraction - concentrically. The joint action taking place is extension and abduction ...*

1. b. *The lever system operating at the elbow during performance is the first class lever system.*

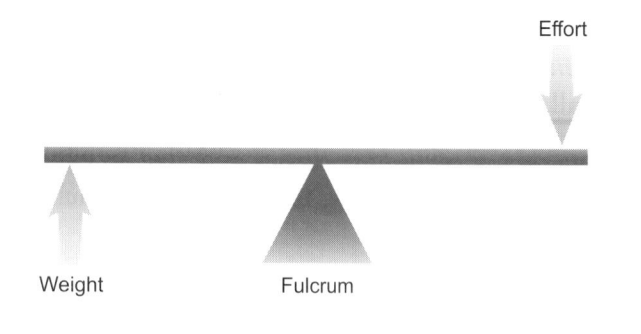

1. c. i. Positive reinforcement is used when something positive happens and thus the outcome is likely to happen again. For example, a player scores a basket and remembers what it felt like.

Negative reinforcement is when something negative happens and you do not want this to occur again. For example, a player misses a basket; negative reinforcement is used so the outcome of this happening again decreases.

Punishment is used when something goes wrong and the performer gets punished. For example, a player misses several shots, is shouted at and brought out of the game.

1. c. ii. Operant conditioning theory is a theory that strengthens the stimulus-response bond so this event is more likely to occur. For example, the coach could set up a specific practice to develop a fast break from a rebound and, if the players score a basket, they receive praise.

Examiner's comment

1. a. *A good, concise answer in which the candidate has achieved maximum marks. Abduction is an incorrect response to the joint action taking place at the elbow; however, as the candidate gave 'extension' first the mark was credited here.*

1. b. *The candidate has successfully stated that the action of shooting involves a first class lever system. It is important to remember that when asked to sketch or draw a diagram, you make the sketch large and ensure that it is clearly labelled – something that this candidate has successfully achieved. Although the candidate has gained full marks for this sketch, there is one small error. Weight always acts downwards and so the arrowhead should be reversed.*

1. c. i. *The student has displayed some knowledge of the terms and used practical examples to illustrate his/her understanding. The first term is awarded two marks as both the explanation and the example are correct. However, the term 'negative reinforcement' is clearly incorrect, a common mistake made by students when explaining this particular term. The final term has been awarded one mark because although the explanation is incorrect or poorly outlined, an appropriate example has been used, which can be credited.*

1. c. ii. *The student has achieved maximum marks for this section. Although the exact terminology in the mark scheme has not been used for the theoretical aspects, it is clear that the student has an understanding of the theoretical concept of operant conditioning. The example outlined is clear and linked to the game of basketball. If another activity had been used this would have been acceptable as the question states 'give an example of how you would use operant learning methods in the coaching of a game such as basketball' – the key words being 'such as'. If the question had requested basketball specifically and another activity had been used, the mark may not have been awarded.*

Unit 2 sample question

2. a. Many people take part in physical recreation as a form of leisure activity.

    i. Define the term 'leisure'. **(2 marks)**

    ii. What do you understand by the term 'physical recreation'? Comment on its benefit to individuals. **(4 marks)**

b. During the late nineteenth century, participation in physical activity within schools was very much determined by social class. With reference to physical activities experienced, contrast the ways in which the upper/middle and working classes were prepared for life after school. **(5 marks)**

c. Outdoor and adventurous activities are one area of activity within the National Curriculum for Physical Education.

    i. Using an example of an activity, identify three educational objectives that outdoor and adventurous activities can provide for pupils. **(3 marks)**

    ii. Why do some people prefer to participate in outdoor and adventurous pursuits as their main leisure activity? **(4 marks)**

(AQA May 2003)

Mark scheme

2. a. i. 1 Time away from/left over after obligations/necessities such as work/education;
2 During which time activities can be freely/voluntarily entered into (choice);
3 For the purpose of relaxation/enjoyment/fun. **(2 marks)**

2. a. ii. 1 Physical recreation – active/exercise/physically strenuous activity;
2 Undertaken during leisure time;
3 Provides opportunities for self-fulfilment/fun/enjoyment/intrinsic reward/improvement of skill;
4 Helps to maintain physical health/fitness;
5 Helps to develop interpersonal/social skills;
6 An escape from reality/pressures/stress. **(any four for 4 marks)**

2. b. Public schools (upper/middle classes) *(max 3 from this section)*
1 Opportunities for team games (suitable examples);
2 To develop Muscular Christianity/Athleticism;
3 To instil values for life/activity for its own sake/fair play/team work/loyalty;
4 To develop specific sport skills for further participation in games;
5 To be played during the extensive amounts of leisure time likely to be available;
6 Development of leadership skills/preparation for leadership roles (suitable examples);
7 Character training.

Elementary schools (working class) *(max 3 from this section)*
8 Provided with drill/therapeutic gymnastics;
9 To develop basic fitness/health;
10 To develop obedience/not to question authority/social control;
11 For preparation for workforce/military service;
12 Limited amount of leisure time likely to be available. **(5 marks)**

2. c. i. 1 Provide achievement for those not succeeding in other activity groups;
2 Avoids direct competition between/against others;
3 Provides a wider range of experiences;
4 Provides a different kind of challenge/element of risk provided by environment;
5 Provides opportunity to discover potential/reach personal limits;
6 Development of leadership;
7 Development of working with others/trust/team building;
8 Development of problem solving/decision making;
9 Develops appreciation/knowledge/understanding of environment;
10 Develops confidence/self-reliance/overcoming fear/survival skills/map and/or compass reading skills;
11 Cross-curricular link with other subjects, for example,

Geography (N.B. use of an appropriate example required for maximum marks). **(any three for 3 marks)**

2. c. ii. 1 Escape from urban life/routine; explore countryside;
2 Seek challenge/risk/thrill/(adrenaline) rush;
3 Influence of PE programme/have developed necessary skills;
4 Influence of media/fashion/role models/youth culture;
5 Away from rules, regulations and strict structure/not competitive;
6 Seek independence/make own decisions/self-paced.
(any four for 4 marks)

Sample answers

2. a. i. Leisure is the spare time we have without obligation [after work is carried out]. An example of a leisure activity would be watching TV. Leisure time is for us to relax and develop as human beings, also as an escape from stress.

2. a. ii. ... the physical recreation is recreational activities, for example, team sports/individual sports [football/tennis], which is played physically using skills and movements to participate with. This benefits individuals in many ways, for example:

to socialise
to develop new skills
to be healthier
to have fun.

2. b. ... working class pupils were brought up in public schools. They were prepared for life through military-based drills. These drills benefited health and fitness and were taught through command style teaching by the class teacher or NCOs. This style encouraged taking orders and required little space.

The upper class and middle class, especially the upper, had the time for sport, so their participation was high. They also had the money for sport. They also had land and facilities that they owned. The upper class would certainly take part in sport in schools. They would have developed their own rules of mob games and then after school would go off to university and take their sports with them. The upper class will have greater knowledge of sport and health. The upper class jobs would consist of doctors, lawyers, diplomatic service and priests.

2. c. i An example of an adventurous activity would be abseiling. Outdoor and adventurous activities provide pupils with an element of danger. These activities encourage teamwork skills, leadership and self-confidence for pupils.

2. c. ii. ... they may have the facilities available, the money to participate in them, they may feel outdoor and adventurous activities provide a challenge. They may thrive for the element of danger. They may fancy a change to traditional sports and feel this promotes good qualities.

Examiner's comment

2. a. i. *Two marks allocated for 'spare time' and 'relax'.*

2. a. ii. *One mark allocated for each of 'using skills', 'to socialise', 'to be healthier' and 'to have fun', achieving the total of 4 marks.*

2. b. *In the first section, the first statement was incorrect but the following sentence was good, so in terms of positive marking the first statement was overlooked and subsequent points were credited. Marks were credited for 'drills', 'health and fitness' and 'taking orders'. This attained the submax of 3, so no more marks could be given for this section.*

The second section on upper/middle classes was too vague to be credited any marks but point 7 was given for reference to the occupations the upper classes would occupy later in life, achieving 4 marks in total.

2. c. i. *The maximum 3 marks were achieved in this section with point 4 given for danger, point 7 for teamwork and point 6 for leadership.*

2. c. ii. *The candidate in this section failed to address the key part of the question, which is basically asking why people prefer these activities, so reference to time and facilities is less relevant. Point 2 on the mark scheme was given for 'challenge', achieving 1 mark.*

Now turn to the AS PE for AQA Student book and try the practice exam questions at the end of each section.